A Social Ecology of Capital

"With *A Social Ecology of Capital*, Éric Pineault provides a remarkably insightful analysis of the complex interface between capital and nature. This is indispensable reading for scholars, students and activists."
—William Carroll, Professor of Sociology,
University of Victoria, Canada

"*A Social Ecology of Capital* is essential reading for all interested in ecological crises, limits to growth, and alternatives. Its materialist-feminist analysis of growth as biophysical expansion and accumulation presents a much-needed foundation for understanding our current predicament."
—Matthias Schmelzer, author of *The Hegemony of Growth*

"A timely and urgent analysis which seeks to comprehend our ecological plight through an elucidation of monopoly capital."
—Gareth Dale, Reader in Political Economy, Brunel University

"In systematically illuminating the material flows and constraints of fossil-fueled capitalism, Pineault has compiled a useful guide to social metabolism for Marxists. He shows that, to understand our global ecological predicament, we must go beyond Marx in establishing a materialist social science."
—Alf Hornborg, Professor Emeritus of Human Ecology,
Lund University and author of *The Magic of Technology:
The Machine as a Transformation of Slavery*

"Social ecology is further developed by Éric Pineault with this fascinating theoretical and empirical study. He shows how capital as a social relation exercises its domination—and how contested this is. A must read for scholars, students, activists, progressive politicians and the interested public!"
—Ulrich Brand, University of Vienna and co-author of *The Imperial
Mode of Living. Everyday Life and the Ecological Crisis of Capitalism*

"Eric Pineault's book is a true *Capital in the 21st Century*. One where ecology matters."
—Giorgos Kallis, ICREA Professor, ICTA-UAB

A Social Ecology of Capital

Éric Pineault

PLUTO PRESS

First published 2023 by Pluto Press
New Wing, Somerset House, Strand, London WC2R 1LA
and Pluto Press Inc.
1930 Village Center Circle, 3-834, Las Vegas, NV 89134

www.plutobooks.com

Copyright © Éric Pineault 2023

The right of Éric Pineault to be identified as the author of this work has been
asserted in accordance with the Copyright, Designs and Patents Act 1988.

British Library Cataloguing in Publication Data
A catalogue record for this book is available from the British Library

ISBN 978 0 7453 4377 8 Paperback
ISBN 978 0 7453 4381 5 PDF
ISBN 978 0 7453 4379 2 EPUB

Typeset by Stanford DTP Services, Northampton, England

Simultaneously printed in the United Kingdom and United States of America

Contents

List of Figures

List of Tables

Acknowledgments

The social ecology of capital as it stands is an unfinished project. I have been able to propose an introductory exploration of the theory and empirics needed to understand the workings and trajectory of the social metabolism of advanced capitalism. I hope the reader will find in this work elements and ideas that will inspire further analysis in a systematic and fruitful direction. I have gathered together strands of research and results from the burgeoning field of the metabolic and biophysical analysis of the economic process, which I have combined with the critical political economy of advanced capitalism in what I hope to be a framework that is both coherent, original and relevant to current socio-ecological struggles. My debt to the Vienna Institute of Social Ecology is immense, they have opened the way for an empirically grounded assessment of the materiality of capitalist accumulation. The data mobilized in this work wouldn't exist without their painstaking and rigorous empirical research as well as the visionary methodological and epistemological advances on which their research is founded. I sincerely hope that my attempt to synthesize their findings inside a critical economic theory of capitalist accumulation contributes to the development of their research program.

My work is also inspired by the activists in Quebec and elsewhere with whom I have worked and stood "shoulder to shoulder and heart to heart"[1] to block, transform and shape the social metabolism of the future in struggles against the construction and promotion of fossil-fuel infrastructures as well as in struggles to define a socially just ecological transition based on the principles of degrowth.

I have written this work haunted by a sentence from Murray Bookchin, to whose memory this book is dedicated. It was during a casual conversation between mentor and student sitting on the porch of a convenience store in Plainfield Vermont in the early 1990s, drinking soda of all things! Every summer young radical ecologists from all over the Americas and elsewhere would converge to study at the Institute of Social Ecology in this

---

1. The words are from Bruce Springsteen's song "We Are Alive," from his album *Wrecking Ball*.

little village lost in the Green Mountains. "Eric, we don't know what capitalism is yet." The sentence later found its way into one of his essays. It was in this way that Bookchin introduced me and others to a dialectical mode of approaching socio-ecological theory. Things are not fixed essences, they become. I guess we will only know in hindsight what capitalism as a social formation was. Bookchin's enigmatic statement is paradoxically for me a beacon of hope. There will be a society which will have experienced and survived a historical trajectory beyond capitalist accumulation and its destructive ecological relations. I hope with this work to have contributed a bit to the collective understanding of this social and ecological formation and to that of its limits. I am very aware that I have not been able to do justice in these pages to Murray's pioneering and essential contribution to the development of social ecology as a critical theory and practice of societal transformation. I hope he would agree that what follows is nevertheless a contribution to his politics of emancipation and is inspired by his dialectics. Of course, I fully assume the shortcomings of what I have been able put together. Parts of this book have been drawn from previously published articles, in particular Chapters 5 and 6 are based on reworked excerpts of "The Ghosts of Progress: Contradictory Materialities of the Capitalist Golden Age,"[2] and the conclusion includes arguments first developed in "The Post-Growth Condition."[3]

This work would not have been possible without the support of Klaus Dorre, Stephen Lessenich, Hartmut Rosa and their companions at the Postwachstumgesellschaften Institute at the University Friedrich Schiller of Jena, Germany. They generously received me and my family during a full year for a sabbatical leave in 2018–2019 where I was able to engage in the fundamental research out of which this book grew. It also grew out of discussions with Dennis Eversberg, Matthias Schmelzer, Emma Dowling, Ulrich Brand and others during this stay in Jena, as well as with researchers at the Institute of Social Ecology in Vienna. I would also like to thank Gareth Dale who closely read and commented on this manuscript, as well as the people at Pluto Press that supported this project throughout its long period of gestation.

2. Éric Pineault, "The Ghosts of Progress: Contradictory Materialities of the Capitalist Golden Age," *Anthropological Theory* 21(3) (2021): 260–286, https://doi.org/10.1177/1463499620980292.
3. Éric Pineault, "The Post-Growth Condition," *Global Dialogue* 9(1) (April 2019): 25–26, https://globaldialogue.isa-sociology.org/articles/the-post-growth-condition.

Introduction

That human societies have ecologies, that they are enmeshed in innumerable ecological relations with a plethora of living beings, that society is embedded materially in ecosystems, is a proposition that one can find in various formulations in all human cultures.[1] Societies actively, passively and in unequal ways, participate in the biogeochemical cycles and ecological processes that make this planet the Earth.[2] They have developed a diversity of languages and modes or representations of these relations and processes.[3] Today, these ecological interdependencies have taken a dramatic turn, scientific assessments of climate change by the Intergovernmental Panel on Climate Change (IPCC), of biodiversity loss by the less-known Intergovernmental Science-Policy Platform on Biodiversity and Ecosystem Services (IPBES)[4] of surpassed or soon to be transgressed planetary boundaries, all point to a trajectory of global, rapid, often irreversible and catastrophic environmental transformation. Catastrophic because the future that is being produced by these geological, ecological and climatic changes will bring about a radically different planet than the Earth that saw the development of human societies since the last glaciation, a planet possibly inhabitable by humans organized in complex

---

1.   This is a central argument developed by the social ecology of Murray Bookchin, in particular in his *Ecology of Freedom: The Emergence and Dissolution of Hierarchy*. Palo Alto, CA: Cheshire Books, 1982. See also Maurice Godelier, *The Mental and the Material: Thought, Economy and Society*. London: Verso,1986; and Philippe Descola, *Beyond Nature and Culture*, trans. Janet Lloyd. Chicago, IL: University of Chicago Press, 2013.
2.   Will Steffen et al., *Global Change and the Earth System: A Planet Under Pressure*. Berlin: Springer, 2004; and for a more recent synthesis, see IPCC, *Climate Change 2021: The Physical Science Basis, Contribution of Working Group I to the Sixth Assessment Report of the Intergovernmental Panel on Climate Change*, Valérie Masson-Delmotte et al. (eds.). Cambridge: Cambridge University Press, 2021. In press. www.ipcc.ch/report/ar6/wg1/.
3.   Descola, *Beyond Nature and Culture*.
4.   For the Intergovernmental Panel on Climate Change, see www.ipcc.ch; and for the Intergovernmental Science-Policy Platform on Biodiversity and Ecosystem Services, see https://ipbes.net.

societies.[5] It is the experience and language of this catastrophic sense of the history of the future that has galvanized ecological movements worldwide and sparked a renewed wave of environmental radicalism in the last ten years.

Among the various struggles and mobilizations that mark this renewal, many directly engage with the materiality of capitalist society: struggles against fossil-fuel infrastructures, struggles against extractivism, whether it be large-scale mining or capitalist appropriation of biomass through plantations and industrial monocultures, struggles to define *just* socio-ecological transformations for workers and communities. To block a continental pipeline project, to successively oppose the construction of major LNG hubs, to shut down—even for only a few minutes—a lignite coal mine, to prevent ecocidal plantations or the felling of old growth forests, to stall or cancel the development of copper, graphite or lithium mines, all are engagements with the future of capitalist metabolism. Engagements that aim to curb the socio-ecological trajectory of the planet by breaking "business as usual" capitalist investments and production.[6] Few of these struggles and movements remain at this negative stage of *Blockadia*,[7] the conditions of struggle themselves involve forging a vision of metabolic relations *that should be* given the existence of planetary and ecological thresholds,[8] in opposition to those *that are* because of

5. Will Steffen et al., "Trajectories of the Earth System in the Anthropocene," Proceedings of the National Academy of Sciences of the United States of America, 115, no. 33 (2018): 8252–8259. www.pnas.org/doi/pdf/10.1073/pnas.1810141115.
6. For a global overview of these struggles, see the Global Atlas of Environmental Justice, https://ejatlas.org.
7. Naomi Klein, *This Changes Everything: Capitalism vs. the Climate*. New York: Simon and Schuster, 2014.
8. The normative aspect of these "envisionings" of socio-ecological change is one of the characteristics that distinguish this contemporary wave of social transformation from New Left and New Social Movements of the late twentieth century with an emancipatory project that focused rather on the "what could be" in tension with the "what is." This tension often involved highlighting how capitalist social relations of exploitation and other relations of domination actively repressed the emancipatory potential of a given level of technological and material development which promised abundance and freedom for all. This was, for example, a central premise of Bookchin's social ecology. For an extensive discussion of this structure of the emancipatory project, see Pierre Charbonnier, *Abondance et liberté: Une histoire environnementale des idées politiques*. Paris: La découverte, 2020. For a discussion of the implications of founding an emancipatory project on self-limitation and an envisioning of what should be, see Ulrich Brand et al., "From Planetary to Societal Boundaries: An Argument for Col-

capitalist development. Depending on locality and context, this can bring together around a common vision of transition broad swathes of society: environmentalists, citizen groups, labor and social justice organizations, first nations and peasant movements, who must all *positively* embrace not only the debate concerning the materiality of society, the need to institute just and viable limits,[9] but also to rethink and rekindle ecological forms of production and reproduction. These struggles, both negative and positive, concern the shape, form and content of the social relations to nature of contemporary societies. Social ecology proposes a language and a system of representation for these struggles. All societies and cultures have the philosophical resources and linguistic capacities needed to represent in a true and creative fashion their social relations to nature,[10] and to critically engage with those relations that capitalist development has imposed. The language of social ecology cannot and should not replace these worldviews or cosmovisions, but it can accompany and nourish their struggles.[11]

ON SOCIAL METABOLISM

The contribution of social ecology to current environmental struggles is a mode of representation of the materiality and ecological relations of capitalist economies as social metabolism. The economic process of human societies in general can be described as a metabolic phenomenon,

---

lectively Defined Self-Limitation," *Sustainability: Science, Practice and Policy* 17(1) (2021): 264–291, https://doi.org/10.1080/15487733.2021.1940754. There are still today movements, groups and activists proposing an emancipatory environmental project based on the twentieth-century pattern of "what could be," some versions of the Green New Deal, as well as self-proclaimed "Accelerationists," for whom any discussion of limits is reactionary and self-defeating. An interesting example can be found in the progressive magazine *Jacobin*'s first engagement with environmental questions in its "Earth, Wind and Fire," *Jacobin* 26 (2017). For an ecomodernist defence of an ecosocialist new green deal, see also Matthew T. Huber, *Climate Change as Class War: Building Socialism on a Warming Planet*. London: Verso, 2022.

9.   Bengi Akbulut and Fikret Adaman, "The Ecological Economics of Economic Democracy," *Ecological Economics* 176 (2020): 106750–106759, https://doi.org/10.1016/j.ecolecon.2020.106750.

10.   Unai Pascual et al. (eds.), "Summary for Policymakers of the Methodological Assessment of the Diverse Values and Valuation of Nature of the Intergovernmental Science-Policy Platform on Biodiversity and Ecosystem Services (IPBES)," Bonn: IPBES (2022), https://doi.org/10.5281/zenodo.6522392.

11.   Brand et al., "From Planetary to Societal Boundaries."

akin to the life processes of singular living beings and subsumed under the same biophysical laws: societies extract and put to work in their economic relations low entropy matter and energy which will eventually dissipate as high entropy wastes, in doing so, they maintain orderly material structures.[12] For living organisms, this metabolic exchange is enmeshed in a web of complex trophic relations where one species' waste is another's food, metabolism is mediated by ecology. For humans, and their economies, this process of metabolic exchange is *also* mediated by social relations, by symbolic structures of meaning, by institutions, ideology and power. Metabolism is a "social ecology."[13] Thus understood, social metabolism is a dialectical category; it exists as mediation: social relations mediate natural processes and natural processes mediate social relations. More specifically, biophysical and social orders of causation *intermediate* each other in the metabolic processes of society.[14] From this standpoint, the current ecological crisis can be approached as contradictory in the sense that prevalent ways and modes of intermediation between biophysical and social processes appear as an aporia for the continued existence of both living nature and society as they exist actually on Earth. The purpose of social ecology, as critical theory, is to explore and explain these ecological contradictions as those of the *economic process* of *capitalist* societies.

We can trace the use of metabolism to understand the materiality and ecology of the economic process all the way back to Marx's analysis of

---

12. Nicholas Georgescu-Roegen, *The Entropy Law and the Economic Process.* Cambridge, MA: Harvard University Press, 1971.

13. Helmut Haberl et al., "Contributions of Sociometabolic Research to Sustainability Science," *Nature Sustainability* 2(3) (2019): 173–184, https://doi.org/10.1038/s41893-019-0225-2.

14. See Christophe Bonneuil and Jean-Baptiste Fressoz, *The Shock of the Anthropocene: The Earth, History and Us*, trans. David Fernbach. London: Verso, 2016. For Jason Moore, this would be a case of "double internality," while an interesting proposal, the author's argument adopts a Latourian ontology that is at odds with a dialectical understanding of nature–society relations developed by social ecology; see Jason W. Moore, *Capitalism in the Web of Life: Ecology and the Accumulation of Capital.* New York: Verso, 2015. Intermediation must not be reduced to conflation, for social ecology, the natural and social orders of causality are autonomous, though in metabolism they are articulated. In this sense, social ecology does mobilize the nature–society binary but in a dialectical and critical realist manner as a duality of properties and not of substances, on this, see Andreas Malm, *The Progress of This Storm: Nature and Society in a Warming World.* London: Verso, 2018.

the labor process in *Capital*.[15] For him, it was labor that mediated the metabolic relations of humans to nature. For social ecology, the range of mediating practices is much wider than what Marx understood as labor, even in a "primal" and transhistorical sense: it encompasses practices of reproduction, care and expressive activities as well as those of production. This limitation cast aside, Marx understood metabolism as the necessary biophysical mediation of societal reproduction—including the biophysical reproduction of human populations. And, as he argued in the *German Ideology*, one must not reduce "reproduction" to mere subsistence requirements and biologically determined needs of humans as living organisms. In Marx's words, "it is a definite form of activity [...], a definite form of expressing their life, a definite *mode of life* [*Lebensweise*] on their part."[16] This insight contains a fundamental methodological principle for our work: the material reproduction of society is oriented by expressive and normative determinations bound together in social relations and symbolic structures.[17] The economic process of human societies is a dialectic of metabolic and symbolic. It cannot be reduced to purely material and biophysical processes, yet, nor can it be reduced to a purely social process of reproduction of symbolic structures, or ideational representations, *in abstracto* of any social relations to nature. *Social* metabolism encompasses both.

Understanding these material relations as "natural" highlights the necessary biophysical transformations that matter and energy undergo as they are mobilized in the economic process of capital and put to work in social relations and practices. Understanding metabolism as "social"

---

15. For a complete genealogical analysis, see Marina Fischer-Kowalski, "Society's Metabolism: The Intellectual History of Materials Flow Analysis, Part I 1860–1970," *Journal of Industrial Ecology* 2(1) (1998): 61–78, https://doi.org/10.1162/jiec.1998.2.1.61.
16. Karl Marx, *The German Ideology*. New York: Prometheus Books, 1998, 37. *Lebensweise* could also be translated as a "way of life."
17. This approach to the socio-symbolic is based on the dialectical sociology of Michel Freitag. Unfortunately, his work is inaccessible in English. The French reader can find in *Dialectique et Société*, Volume 2 "Introduction à une théorie générale du symbolique," and Volume 3 "Contrôle, pouvoir et contrôle," elements of the sociological theory that forms the backdrop of this work; see Michel Freitag, *Introduction à une théorie générale du symbolique: dialectique et société*, Vol. 2. Montreal: Liber, 2011; and Michel Freitag, Culture, pouvoir, contrôle: les modes de reproduction formels de la société. dialectique et société, Vol. 3. Montreal: Liber, 2013. Familiarity with this theory is not needed to follow the sociological argument present in this book.

highlights the fact that these transformations are directed and mediated by significant practices. They are purposeful and expressive, though the biophysical impact and ecological consequences of extraction, accumulation and waste might not be intended or desired. And they come together as a totality, characterizing society as a whole in the form of distinctive and historical "metabolic regimes."

In this dialectical tradition, social metabolism is more than a metaphor, it designates the real biophysical process of societal reproduction through purposeful, instituted, economic relations. This realist stance implies that the individual metabolic activity of human beings—as biological organisms—is itself subsumed and mediated by the totality that is social metabolism. It could be argued that there are as many forms of social metabolism as there are societies. Social ecologists and environmental historians have proposed a typology distinguishing three great metabolic regimes that encompass the totality of social forms that have existed up until this day: hunting-gathering societies, agrarian societies and fossil-industrial societies. A typology that is rather classical, and, one could argue, that reflects the self-understanding of modern Western capitalist societies (or their elites) looking back in a skewed and biased way on their own trajectory. Built on the "claim that the energy system represents the most basic constraint for the differentiation of socio-ecological systems,"[18] it speaks to societies that have made the extraction, distribution and work of physical energy carriers a foundational structure of their metabolism: capitalist societies. And the typology is useful precisely because it highlights their historical singularity, how in this metabolic regime, biophysical surpluses are extracted and accumulated, how the instituted relation between biophysical surplus and value reifies the growth process and gives rise to novel ecological contradictions.

It was Marx who originally developed the category of metabolism to understand the labor process, but he did not develop a metabolic analysis of capitalist society as a whole, or the categories necessary for the task as it is needed today. One can interpret passages on capitalist agriculture in Books I and III of *Capital* as what we would today understand as an

---

18. Fridolin Krausmann, Marina Fischer-Kowalski, Heinz Schandl and Nina Eisenmenger, "The Global Sociometabolic Transition: Past and Present Metabolic Profiles and their Future Trajectories," *Journal of Industrial Ecology* 12(5–6) (2008): 639, https://doi.org/10.1111/j.1530-9290.2008.00065.x.

exposé of the ecological contradictions of large-scale capitalist agriculture. Based on these occurrences, as well as others, John Bellamy Foster
and his colleagues, Paul Burkett and Kohei Saito, have presented in many
lengthy volumes what they consider to be Marx's ecological critique of
capitalism.[19] That Marx today would have probably been an "ecologist"
and that he would have developed a radical environmental critique of
capitalism is an interesting speculative proposition. That, furthermore,
Marx and Engels closely followed the development of thermodynamics,
agronomy, chemistry, evolutionary theory and other natural sciences
that today form the basis of the metabolic analysis of societies and of the
environmental sciences is of interest to understand the development of
Marxian theory. That the critique developed in *Capital* is not inherently
anti-ecological or productivist and even contains important concepts
for a Marxist or Marxian critical theory of the ecological relations of
capital—such as the concept of the metabolic rift—is a very important
result of the detailed studies they have produced.[20] Finally, that Marx, in
taking into account the metabolic dimension of capitalism, in particular
during his study of the labor process, avoided the trap of reducing
social relations to biophysical processes (see, for example, the critique
of Podolinsky's "energy" theory of value) is an important lesson for the
development of an ecological critique of capitalism.[21] But, as argued by
Andreas Malm, ecology and the analysis of the biophysical scale of the

19. Kohei Saito, *Karl Marx's Ecosocialism: Capital, Nature, and the Unfinished
Critique of Political Economy*. New York: Monthly Review Press, 2017; John Bellamy
Foster, Brett Clark and Richard York, *The Ecological Rift: Capitalism's War on the Earth*.
New York: Monthly Review Press, 2010; John Bellamy Foster and Brett Clark, *The
Robbery of Nature: Capitalism and the Ecological Rift*. New York: Monthly Review
Press, 2020; Paul Burkett, *Marx and Nature: A Red Green Perspective*. Chicago, IL:
Haymarket Books, 2014; and Paul Burkett and John Bellamy Foster, *Marx and the
Earth: An Anti-Critique*. Chicago, IL: Haymarket Books, 2019; among others.
20. In his recent work, Timothée Haug has critiqued and questioned part of this
interpretive work showing how it is based on a selective and decontextualized
reading of certain passages of Marx's writings. For Haug, one must distinguish Marx
the "strategic productivist" before 1863 and Marx a "cautious ecologist" during the
writing of *Capital*. Our book not being an intervention in the field of Marxology and
the hermeneutics of Marx's writings, we will leave this question to those philosophers
and historians of social theory equipped to debate these questions with the necessary
theoretical and linguistic skills.
21. Paul Burkett and John Bellamy Foster, "Metabolism, Energy, and Entropy in
Marx's Critique of Political Economy: Beyond the Podolinsky Myth," *Theory and
Society* 35 (2006): 109–156, https://doi.org/10.1007/s11186-006-6781-2.

capitalist process were not central aspects of Marx's critical work.[22] An ecologized materialism was simply not Marx's epistemic project, though it might be the episteme we need today. Biophysical and ecological processes do not appear as *central* determinations in Marx's understanding of the laws or tendencies that governed the development of capitalism in his day. Because of his polemical relation to Malthus, he was very wary of an integration of the concept of natural limits in the categorial system of the critique of capitalism.[23] Metabolic rifts remain secondary aspects in his theory. Nature as "use-values" is present in *Capital*, but Marx did not develop in this work a distinctive critical vocabulary that could express biophysical and ecological determinations of the capitalist economic process in a systematic manner. So, if his work, *Capital* in particular, is a necessary point of departure for an ecological critique of capitalist metabolism, the critique must move beyond Marx, in search of categories that can aptly express social metabolism in a systematic fashion.[24]

A century after Marx, in the 1970s, as the ecological contradictions of advanced capitalism[25] came to the fore, the ecological and biophysical language of stocks and flows, of sources and sinks, of a large and entropic throughput sustaining a much smaller value bearing output, was developed by "biophysical" economists such as Nicholas Georgescu-Roegen. This emerging critical perspective proposed a shift of analysis from

22. Andreas Malm, "For a Fallible and Lovable Marx: Some Thoughts on the Latest Book by Foster and Burkett," *Critical Historical Studies* 4(2) (Fall 2017): 267–275, https://doi.org/10.1086/693903.
23. On this, see Timothée Haug, *La Rupture écologique dans l'œuvre de Marx, Analyse d'une métamorphose inachevée du paradigme de la production*, PhD thesis in philosophy, University of Strasbourg, 2022.
24. Paul Burkett's *Marxism and Ecological Economics: Toward a Red and Green Political Economy* (Leiden: Brill, 2006) is an early and useful attempt to engage with non-Marxian approaches to the metabolism of capitalist economies. Unfortunately, apart from a few papers on the "Podolinsky affair" and a polemic with Joan Martinez-Alier, it seems this attempt to synthesize and critically integrate findings and theories from other heterodox schools of the political economy of advanced capitalism was abandoned by the rift school in favor of a "return to Marx." This is all the more surprising given the excellent earlier work produced by John Bellamy Foster on the theory of monopoly capitalism which does engage with post-Keynesian and Kaleckian approaches to capitalism and contains a critique of Marxist fundamentalism. In the latter part of this book, we have drawn extensively from this very same theoretical corpus and Bellamy Foster's work was a useful guide into this field.
25. The expression "advanced capitalism" will be defined later in this introduction.

the internal contradictions of capitalism to its external limits. But doing so implied that the framework developed to understand exploitation as a relation of surplus extraction through social domination was dropped, explicitly so by Georgescu-Roegen in his magnus opus *The Entropy Law and the Economic Process*.[26] The language of biophysical scale sufficed for Georgescu-Roegen to explain what appeared as natural limits to the economic process. For a social ecology of capital, this language is as incomplete as Marx's. Absolute and relative biophysical scale are effectively very powerful conceptual tools that can express the size of the economy which commands a throughput that creates unsustainable forcings both in source and sink interfaces between society and nature. Tools that can express growth rates which exacerbate these forcings and create new ones, and the accumulation rate of stocks that lock in ever-higher throughput rates. In this language, the materiality of capitalist metabolism appears as an escalatory phenomenon.

These concepts and empirical realities form the core of the first part of this book on capitalist metabolism. We have explored them by drawing on contemporary Social Ecology as developed primarily in Vienna. The Vienna Institute of Social Ecology, ever since the foundational article by Marina Fischer-Kowalski and Helmut Haberl, "Tones, Joules and Money,"[27] has further developed the conceptual and empirical tools needed to understand the biophysical scale of contemporary societies and their ecological implications.[28]

From this perspective, the *materiality* of capitalist metabolism appears in one of three guises: social metabolism as *flows of energy and matter passing through societies*, or *throughput*; social metabolism as *an accumulation of material stocks*; and social metabolism as the *colonization of ecosystems by human activity*.

26. Nicholas Georgescu-Roegen, *The Entropy Law and the Economic Process*. Cambridge, MA: Harvard University Press, 1971.
27. Marina Fischer-Kowalski and Helmut Haberl, "Tons, Joules, and Money: Modes of Production and Their Sustainability Problems," *Society and Natural Resources* 10(1) (1997): 61–85, https://doi.org/10.1080/08941929709381009.
28. Johanna Kramm et al., "Societal Relations to Nature in Times of Crisis—Social Ecology's Contributions to Interdisciplinary Sustainability Studies," *Sustainability* 9(7) (2017): 1042, https://doi.org/10.3390/su9071042.

Social Metabolism as Flows of Energy and Matter Passing Through Societies, or Throughput

Throughput is a basic and foundational category of social ecology. As that which passes through society, it is neither the economic output, nor is it a sum of "use-values" with natural properties that answer human needs. It refers to the biophysical flow of elements—energy, lifeforms and organized matter—from source to sink that societies transform to reproduce their constitutive structures. The emphasis on biophysical transformation is central to the concept of throughput and sets it apart from economic theories based on the notion of production and value: if value can be produced, matter can only be transformed. Furthermore, the throughput perspective extends the standard two-stage models of the economy where production and consumption are coupled one to another, to four stages: extraction, industrial transformation, consumptive transformation and dissipation as waste. The throughput must be extracted or harvested from biogeochemical sources and it will be absorbed by biogeochemical sinks as waste once it has gone through a series of successive entropic transformations mediated by labor and consumptive activities. This flow can be measured quantitatively as the mass or energy content of various elements and qualitatively in terms of its composition. Finally, if the throughput is linear from the standpoint of social metabolism, it is necessarily part of wider ecological and biogeochemical cycles which are not. The ecological contradictions of capital appear precisely at these points of friction where a linear social process forces cyclical natural processes.

An obvious example is the carbon cycle which has been forced and accelerated by the massive extraction and combustion of fossil fuels during the last two centuries in the advanced capitalist core. But the same can be said of other critical biogeochemical cycles of the Earth system such as nitrogen and phosphorous, essential inputs in industrial agriculture.[29] In the case of nitrogen, anthropogenic flows surpassed natural nitrogen fixation in terrestrial ecosystems in the 1980s,[30] the ecolog-

---

29. For a critical political ecology approach to these cycles, see Matt Huber's interesting analysis in "Reinvigorating Class in Political Ecology: Nitrogen Capital and the Means of Degradation," *Geoforum* 85 (October 2017): 345–352, https://doi.org/10.1016/j.geoforum.2017.01.010.

30. William Battye, Viney P. Aneja and William H. Schlesinger, "Is Nitrogen the Next Carbon?" *Earth's Future* 5(9) (2017): 894–904, https://doi.org/10.1002/2017EF000592.

ical consequences of the mass dissipation of these flows has taken the form of increased eutrophication of coastal waters and the appearance of dead zones in areas such as the Gulf of Mexico and Lake Erie in North America.[31] A much less debated issue are the mass flows of sand and aggregates associated with the cement and infill needed for the construction of buildings and infrastructures (highways, dams, bridges and landscape management) that are the hallmarks of modern urbanized space. As we shall see in Chapter 1, extraction rates of these materials are following an exponential growth rate and the proportion they represent in the overall metabolism of human societies amounts today to almost 50 percent. The extraction and disposal of these materials is not without ecological consequences, the formation of sand results from geological processes of erosion that have a slow temporality entirely disconnected from current extractive practices. Extraction rates are estimated to be 32 to 50 billion tonnes per year while sediment transport by the world's rivers is estimated to be 20 billion tonnes per year. Furthermore, sand-based terrestrial, river and marine landscapes such as deltas and beaches are essential abiotic structures that support many unique ecosystems and sand-based geomorphology is essential to the mitigation of floods in coastal zones and floodplains. Contemporary sand extraction is destroying many of these ecosystems and landscapes all the while enhancing the fragility of coastal built environments, and on top of this, certain regions of the world are experiencing exhaustion of locally available sand resources.[32] We could continue exploring other aspects of the materiality of contemporary societies, and will do so in Chapter 1, but here, to put the argument in more general terms, mass production and mass consumption, two salient features of advanced capitalism, imply mass extraction, mass flows of matter and mass dissipation of waste. Throughput captures this aspect of the materiality of capitalist metabolism and is a necessary first step in unveiling its ecological contradictions. Its language of gigatonnes, gigajoules, of mass flows of brute matter is certainly not

31. Robert J. Diaz and Rutger Rosenberg, "Spreading Dead Zones and Consequences for Marine Ecosystems," *Science* 321(5891) (2008): 926–929, https://doi.org/10.1126/science.1156401.
32. Robert John, "Sand Geographies: Disentangling the Material Foundations of the Built Environment," *Geography Compass* 15(5) (2021): e12560, https://doi.org/10.1111/gec3.12560.

very poetic, but this does reflect essential features of the logic of advanced capitalism: massified, abstract and not so poetic.

Social Metabolism as an Accumulation of Material Stocks

In any given society, elements of the throughput coalesce into structures, be they bodies, human or animal, as well as the material artifacts (machines, buildings, SUVs, appliances, tools, toys and e-gadgets) that populate the capitalist world. In the language of social ecology, all are conceptualized as "stocks," but in mass terms, manufactured and built artifacts dwarf bodies, by the human or non-human, in capitalist society. Our work will thus focus on these artifacts or material stocks. At a very abstract level, in any given society, material and energy flows are needed to maintain these stocks. Just as capitalism's growth spiral has expanded the material throughput to sustain the existence of an ever-larger mass of commodified output, it has also grown the mass of material stocks. And because of their existence as structures, the more they accumulate, the more flows they command. Thus, stocks command flows, from the initial building up of stocks out of flows, to the sustaining flows and eventually replacement flows as well as waste flows to sinks. Stocks lock-in flows in diverse ways in capitalist societies, these lock-ins are of course material, but they are also social as habits, practice and social power coalesce around certain stock forms. This flow lock-in exacerbates the ecological contradictions of the mass throughput of capitalist metabolism. Yet, from the standpoint of social theory, the category of material stocks amalgamates objects that are determined by radically different social relations; one of the tasks and challenges of a critical social ecology is to reintroduce the language of social domination and property relations to understand how capital is embodied in certain stocks: *capitalized artifacts*; and mediates the formation of others as *commodified artifacts*.

Examples of artifacts that command flows are all around us, be they the simplest of household appliances or e-devices that organize the reproduction of our daily lives, to more complex and massive machines such as cars and SUVs. These exist in a nexus of commodified social relations. These can be contrasted with "productive" and "extractive" artifacts such as pipelines, refineries, industrial machine tools and shopping centers which have been capitalized and must generate a return through productive use from the standpoint of capital. In an advanced capitalist economy, most capitalized artifacts are controlled by large monopolistic corporations which preside over their production through investment, useful life through production and destruction through depreciation. These moments are not primarily determined by the physical use or material performance of these artifacts but by the imperative of valorization that drives the accumulation of capital by corporations.[33] Finally, many artifacts also exist in the public realm as state property in the form of collectively used infrastructure: roads, public transit systems such as metros and trains, sewer systems and waste treatment plants. Though not subject to a valorization imperative *per se*, they do exist as important preconditions that enable capitalist accumulation and they also provide fixes for capital accumulation either as a sink for capitalist savings or as impetus for capitalist production during cyclical economic downturns.[34]

Social Metabolism as the Colonization of Ecosystems by Human Activity

The production of hybrid and socialized ecosystems, often simpler and less resilient, sometimes leading to new artificialized spaces and biophysical structures which—in analogous manner to stocks—can only be maintained by high throughput rates. Because of their hybrid nature, these ecosystems can develop into unexpected and sometimes problematic structures from a societal standpoint and thus command further interventions. Such is the case of those fields, wetlands and forests that have been transformed into intensive high-input industrial agroecosystems. But such is also the case of sprawled urban megalopolises with their water management, waste management and heat management problems.

For social ecology, there can be no "output" of goods and services, no build-up of productive capacity in "inputs" or fixed capital, no enjoyment of use-values, without a throughput of energy and matter, the accumu-

---

33. Anke Schaffartzik et al., "The Transformation of Provisioning Systems from an Integrated Perspective of Social Metabolism and Political Economy: A Conceptual Framework," *Sustainability Science* 16(5) (2021): 1405–1421, https://doi.org/10.1007/s11625-021-00952-9.

34. Michael Ekers and Scott Prudham, "The Metabolism of Socioecological Fixes: Capital Switching, Spatial Fixes, and the Production of Nature," *Annals of the American Association of Geographers* 107(6) (2017): 1370–1388, https://doi.org/10.1080/24694452.2017.1309962.

lation of stocks and without the colonization of ecosystems. These three dimensions come together in the form of historical metabolic regimes which can be examined at various levels of abstraction and generality. Capitalism is not a metabolic regime per se, its development has been articulated to two regimes that we will explore successively, agrarian metabolic regimes and fossil-industrial metabolic regimes.

From the above insights, we will derive and unfold the following propositions concerning the material dimension of capitalist societies: 1. output—the goods and services commodified in capitalism—implies throughput; 2. the throughput is generated or extracted and sunk into colonized ecosystems with varying degrees of hybridity and artificialization, these command their own throughput flows; 3. throughput flows define the boundary between society and nature; 4. the mass and nature of the stocks in a given economy define the intensity and quality of the throughput; and 5. finally, because capitalism is a monetary production economy, in a capitalist society, throughput flows are veiled and stocks appear as "inherently productive" privately held fixed capital or durable consumer goods, veiling their throughput dependence through what Alf Hornborg has theorized as technological fetishism.[35] Social ecology has developed analytical tools that unveil these biophysical processes.

The purpose of the social ecology of capital is to propose a synthesis between this biophysical analysis of the metabolic foundations of capitalist societies and wider theories of capitalism able to explain the social relations that govern the monetary production economy. In a way, the analytical effort aims to re-sociologize many of the categories and insights developed by social ecology, moving from the idea of social metabolism in the abstract to the social metabolism of capitalist societies. And thus, how capital as an instituted social structure and relation shapes and defines the metabolism of contemporary societies in a way that generates the ecological contradictions which they now face is our project. But for this to be a truly socio-ecological analysis, biophysical and ecological processes and structures must retain their causality in the overall explanation. Capital has a social ecology: it mediates the metabolism of contemporary societies, and as in any mediated process, it is also determined by that which it mediates.

---

35. Alf Hornborg, *Nature, Society, and Justice in the Anthropocene: Unraveling the Money-Energy-Technology Complex*. Cambridge: Cambridge University Press, 2019.

INTRODUCTION

THEORIES OF CAPITAL AND ACCUMULATION

Capital is not a thing; it is a social relation. Things—money, financial assets, inventories of unsold commodities, tools, machines, buildings and landed property or brands and patents—are forms taken by capital in a process of continuous metamorphosis. Taken in isolation, none of these reifications of capital capture its essence, though each is a manifestation—in the eyes of capitalists and others—of its existence as an objective social and economic force. In the Marxian tradition, behind these forms, lies a fundamental social relation: the exploitation of wage labor which produces surplus value.[36] The essence of capital is dual, on the one hand its existence implies the subsumption of productive activity as wage labor, and on the other hand emerges from the productive process of society a surplus that takes on a "value-form." Across history, and in most corners of the planet, one can find instances of capitalist activity that pre-exist the subsumption of the economic process of society by capital. In the guise of merchants, traders, petty producers, planters and speculators, capital has existed alongside other economic forms of subsistence, appropriation and circulation. In some instances, these economic activities can profoundly transform societies and their ecological relations. They can impose modes of life dependent on market, money and trade that penetrate deep into the fabric of society; they can also lead to vast accumulations of money capital and to long circuits of international trade spanning oceans and uniting continents in commercial empires such as during the first phase of the Ming dynasty in China or on smaller and less significative scales in classical imperial Athens or Renaissance Venice. We follow Marx and Polanyi in considering these societies as not being capitalist, which does not mean that they are not bereft of relations of social domination and exploitation, but that they do not have a capitalist form.

An often-cited characteristic of capitalist society is the centrality of markets in their economic process. This can mean the mediation of subsistence needs and provisioning of basic and necessary goods and services by self-regulating, price making markets. And though this is a common feature of capital's domination over the economic process, in a truly

---

36. This argument is most clearly expressed by Marx in his essay titled: "Revenue and its Sources. Vulgar Political Economy," that was added as an addendum to the "Theories of Surplus Value," (1862–1863), edited by Karl Kautsky (1905–1910).

capitalist society market dependance extends its constraint beyond consumption goods and services. It is also more than a constraint imposed on petty producers as a necessary outlet for autonomously produced goods and services. The above features could characterize a market society and economy that need not be capitalist and certainly not necessarily organized according to a capitalist class structure. Are capitalist societies where the market constraint mediates the existence of productive activity as labour power in relations of class domination. Following the work of Franck Fischbach,[37] we wish to insist on the expressive dimension of the class relation of domination specific to capitalism. Of course, this class relation implies the separation between direct producers and the means of production. This relation is organized by capitalist social property relations which concern land, tools, machinery and raw materials as well as intermediate inputs, all provisioned by means of markets. But Fischbach insists on the sociological feature which has important consequences for social ecology: it creates a class of potential producers *who cannot autonomously mobilize in the given institutionalized social relations their labor power*, nor can they access means of subsistence outside of the market. They cannot "express" their capacity to produce a given way of life. This expressive capacity is monopolized by those who exercise the relation of domination of capital over labor; they are in a position to decide how the social division of labor will evolve, how the capacity to produce will be directed and who is included and excluded from capitalist productive activity.

In capitalism, this social condition is not an interstitial feature of social life and does not concern marginal swathes of society; it is a general and ever-expanding social condition. To put it more succinctly, a capitalist social formation in this work is one where not only is the commodification of "things" prevalent, not only are market exchange opportunities institutionalized, but also one where commodified labor power is a central institution of social integration. In such a society, one class, capitalists, will find a market of "freed" labor power that can be bought in exchange for money and another class, laborers, will be constrained to sell their labor power to work and gain their means of subsistence in the form of *monied* wages.

---

37. Franck Fischbach, *La privation de monde: temps, espace et capital: problèmes et controverses*. Paris: J. Vrin, 2011.

Monetary integration where expenditures become revenues and revenues become expenditures in a web of monetary circuits is an essential macroeconomic feature of capitalism as a social form. Too often the definition of capital is reduced to a simple valorization and ensuing commodification process, but for capital to become a general mediation of societal reproduction and for it to subsume the economic process of society as a whole, it must also institutionalize a sphere of realization where what is produced and bears value is bought and consumed.[38] This macroeconomic integration of the economic process of capital need not adopt the contours of the nation state, though it often has because historically the monetary integration of modern capitalist societies depends on state money or the state guarantee of bank money.[39] The degree of dependence of a given society on this process of realization for the provisioning of means of subsistence and flourishing, determines to a large extent its capitalist nature. *Capital* exists and deploys its logic of accumulation and commodification in many social formations, but *capitalism* as a social form emerges when the monetary circuits of capital embrace and enmesh the whole of society, the structures of daily life and determine their reproduction.[40]

38. This perspective, first put forward by Rosa Luxemburg in her *The Accumulation of Capital* (1913), was further developed by Michał Kalecki and theorists of capitalism as a Monetary Production Economy such as Antonio Graziani, will be the framework adopted here. For an overview, see Riccardo Bellofiore (ed.), *Rosa Luxemburg and the Critique of Political Economy*. London: Routledge, 2009.
39. Geoffrey Ingham, *The Nature of Money: New Directions in Political Economy*. Cambridge: Polity Press, 2004.
40. Was the slave plantation economy of the Caribbean critical to the formation of capitalism in Europe and Great Britain in particular? Yes, this was established by Eric Williams in the 1940s and reaffirmed by world systems theorists in the 1970s. As argued by Luxemburg, capitalist accumulation thrives through its articulation to non-capitalist and semi-capitalist social formation, the slave plantation system is a case in point. Economically it maximizes the extortion of labor time and abstract labor power while pushing to a minimum the economic cost—for the capitalist—of the reproduction of labor power. This same logic applies to the plantation as an agro-ecological system of net primary production. Yet, a slave plantation *economy* would rapidly face effective demand and output absorption problems, tendentially monetary exchange would shrink to the strict minimum needed to cover inputs and even these could be appropriated in non-monetized relations. In the end, in such an economy, surplus need not take on a monetary form and the constraint to invest a monetary surplus in the further expansion of productive activity would be replaced by other forms of surplus absorption and manifestations of social domination and privilege. Colonialism does not have to be capitalist to be brutal, exploitative, violent and eco-

Capital, as it exists as a core mediation of the economic process of capitalist social formations, is defined by the subsumption of productive activity as wage labor and by the production of an output and economic surplus that has a value-form. Let us examine in turn each of these determinations, in light of some recent contributions to the critique of capitalism as an economic process.

Capital transforms productive activity by subsuming it as wage labor; this is the first proposition. Wage labor does not exist in and of itself, nor for that manner does "productive activity" as something separate and distinguishable from the flux of daily life activities. Classical political economists were obsessed with the distinction between productive and unproductive labor, a problem that Marx discussed during hundreds of pages in his *Theories of Surplus Value*. Contemporary feminist critiques of capitalism, in particular materialist reproduction theory, have displaced this discussion in a most fecund manner. We draw here on a tradition inaugurated by Rosa Luxemburg in *The Accumulation of Capital* (1913) and pursued by Maria Mies in the 1980s and her feminist colleagues of the Bielefeld school of ecofeminism.[41] Capital mediates social activity by separating productive and reproductive labor: the first being valued, mobilized as work and exchanged for wages in what becomes a productive sphere; and the second is devalued as housework and provisioning activities in what becomes a reproductive sphere of unpaid but necessary care and labor. Reproductive labor and care refer to those activities necessary for the reproduction of social life—which encompasses the biological reproduction of human populations. This separation is gendered and

---

logically destructive. But slave plantation systems articulated to the expansive logic of a capitalist social formation like Great Britain during Industrial Revolution such as the sugar plantations of the Caribbean and the cotton plantation of the southern United States, took on capitalist characteristics. Moreover, the specific socio-ecological conditions of exploitation of the slave plantation system and its coloniality were crucial to the production on a massive and exponentially growing scale of essential inputs to British industrial capitalism during this crucial phase of accumulation. Cotton production in particular could not have expanded at a speed compatible with the accumulation of British capital in the textile sector without the dual context of the colonial relation to land and slavery in the southern United States plantation economy. On this, see the excellent study by Sven Beckert, *Empire of Cotton: A Global History*. New York: Vintage Press, 2015.

41. Tove Soiland, "A Feminist Approach to Primitive Accumulation," in Judith Dellheim and Frieder Otto Wolf (eds.), *Rosa Luxemburg: A Permanent Challenge for Political Economy*. London: Palgrave Macmillan, 2008.

spatialized, capitalist workplaces emerge as distinct spaces from domestic spaces, and valued work is progressively displaced from the household, while life-making reproductive activities are progressively bound to this space. Traditional definitions of capitalist exploitation are built around the separation between the bearers of labor power and the means of production that mediate their capacity to work, from this division originates the proletarian condition. Social reproduction theory shifts this definition toward a theory of a double separation, capital emerges by separating labor power from the means of production and by isolating labor power from the necessary labor of reproduction, so that inside a capitalist society some labor is valued as productive because other forms of labor are devalued as reproductive. And this is organized along a gendered boundary of domination.

Production and reproduction co-evolve in a dialectic throughout the trajectory of capitalist social formations,[42] their relation is fraught with tensions and unresolved contradictions between life-affirming and value-producing social activity. Capital draws surplus value and value *tout court* from productive labor, yet it depends on the existence of a reproductive life-affirming sphere of care that it cannot produce. Reproductive activities themselves can shift from the unpaid to paid and waged status in a continuum that sees some forms of care labor absorbed by the productive sphere of surplus value or diverted to the public sector of "unproductive"— from the standpoint of capital—but necessary waged labor.[43]

The tensions that arise from capital's imperative of valorization is redoubled by tensions that arise from the imperative of realization of value. As discussed earlier, a capitalist social formation is distinguished not only because commodification runs rampant and processes of valorization of capital absorb and appropriate social activity as labor as well as commons and nature as inputs (in Marxian terms variable and constant capital), but also because a capitalist social formation comes together as a totality through macroeconomic closure: when production is validated and realized through the consumption of the valued output. In this moment of realization, wages return to capitalists in the form of

42. Maria Mies, *Patriarchy and Accumulation on a World Scale: Women in the International Division of Labor*. London: Zed Books, 1986.
43. Emma Dowling, *The Care Crisis: What Caused It and How Can We End It?* London: Verso, 2022.

market income and surplus value recoups its monetary form, ready for a new bout of expanded capitalist production.[44] And just as the production of surplus value depends on the transformation of social activity into abstract labor, the realization of produced value depends on the subsumption of the reproductive sphere and its gendered activities. Market dependance for subsistence, provisioning and flourishing, while leaving the form and content of reproductive activities autonomous from capital, corresponds to formal subsumption; commodification and colonization of the lifeworld through the development of cultures of "consumption" correspond to the real subsumption of the reproductive sphere. As social reproduction theorists explain, this process of subsumption is never complete, the autonomy of life-affirming activities is an immanent sociological property of human existence.[45]

By consumption, then, we refer to the social phenomena that result from the contradictory process of subsumption of reproductive activities, social provisioning and the reproductive sphere by capital in its process of realization of value. Mass consumption patterns that emerged after World War Two in advanced capitalist social formations such as in North America correspond to a deep and radical transformation of reproductive activities, to a spatial reconfiguration of the reproductive sphere and a redefinition of what "life-affirming" meant by the promotion of a consumption driven lifestyles.[46] This was not a unilateral affair; it was contested throughout the post-war era and remains today by countercultures, from Hippies to Degrowth, and more mundane forms of resistance such as the persistence of uncommodified practices of subsistence, care and commoning. To sum up: the productive sphere of capital depends on an autonomous reproductive sphere it cannot produce and from which it draws unpaid and necessary services, but the productive sphere of capital continuously expands into this reproductive sphere in search of labor to be waged for valorization or care and subsistence activities that can absorb the commodified output of capitalist production. Consumption refers in this perspective to those reproductive activities that are market

44. Augusto Graziani, *The Monetary Theory of Production*. Cambridge: Cambridge University Press, 2003.
45. Gargi Bhattacharyya, *Rethinking Racial Capitalism: Questions of Reproduction and Survival*. London: Rowman & Littlefield, 2018.
46. Susan Strasser, *Waste and Want: A Social History of Trash*. New York: Metropolitan Books, 1999.

INTRODUCTION

dependent and mediated by capitalistically produced commodities;[47] the degree of mediation or subsumption can vary from weak to strong, all the while never being total because of the radical expressive autonomy of life-affirming social reproduction.[48]

The colonization and subsumption of the gendered sphere of reproduction is a necessary yet impossible tendency of capitalist accumulation, necessary both as a source of unpaid labor and services that cheapens the cost of paid labor in the valorization process and necessary as a sphere outside of production that can absorb the capitalist output and realize the produced value. But as highlighted strongly by Luxemburg, this capacity to absorb the output is only possible under the macroeconomic condition that households have the necessary monetary income to validate capitalist production through their consumption. Before the mid-twentieth century, this was at best a shaky and fragile equilibrium,[49] capitalism was subject to regular overproduction and underconsumption crises. What has become known as Fordism, a mode of regulation based on wage-led growth, saw the emergence in the advanced capitalist core of a wide stratum of laboring households able to absorb the constant surplus production generated by capital accumulation.[50]

Following the tradition rooted in the economics of Rosa Luxemburg and kept alive by the Bielefeld school of ecofeminism,[51] we can understand the relation between capital and reproduction as a boundary,[52] and

---

47. I insist on the capitalist context of production to acknowledge the existence of commodities that can be brought to market by non-capitalist producers, including workers co-ops and independent producers. The consumptive norm embedded in these objects is not subject to the same determinations as those objects produced by capitalist enterprise, monopolistic corporations in particular.
48. Stefania Barca, *Forces of Reproduction: Notes for a Counter-Hegemonic Anthropocene*. Cambridge: Cambridge University Press, 2020.
49. The narrower the class of waged workers, the shakier the equilibrium, the more growth prospects and accumulation possibilities for capital are constrained.
50. On this, see Michel Aglietta, *A Theory of Capitalist Regulation: The US Experience*. London: Verso, 2000; and a recent discussion of this work can be found in Éric Pineault, "The Ghosts of Progress: Contradictory Materialities of the Capitalist Golden Age," *Anthropological Theory* 21(3) (2021): 260–286, https://doi.org/10.1177/1463499620980292.
51. For an overview, see Soiland, "A Feminist Approach to Primitive Accumulation," 185.
52. This has also been a theme strongly developed by Nancy Fraser in the last decade, for example, in Nancy Fraser, "Contradictions of Capital and Care," *New Left Review*

define the latter's expansionary drive as bounded by frontiers which articulate capitalist dynamics to other social processes and forms. This is a wider and more general argument that can be useful to analyze the articulations between capitalist accumulation and colonization, slavery and racialization, as well as gendered forms of domination as proposed by Marie Mies in her works.[53] Keeping the reproductive sphere and its consumptive frontier in focus, we can now highlight the implications for the study of capitalist metabolism from the perspective of a critical social ecology. In the formal language of material and energy flow analysis, the consumption patterns and practices of households are key determinants and drivers of both biophysical flows and the accumulation of material stocks. Instead of attributing the cause of consumption to unproblematic "household preferences," we can situate them in the field of contradictory social forces outlined above and we have the critical tools to analyze these determining structures of capitalist metabolism.

The second proposition concerns the nature of value and surplus: capital is defined by the production of an output and surplus that has a value-form. To qualify the output of the economic process and its surplus as having a value-form is to situate these in the conceptual space of a monetary production economy. In this space, output and surplus are produced first as commodities and then, once sold, exist as money flowing back into the coffers of capitalist producers. We could delve into the intricacies of the labor theory of value (or as aptly expressed by Bellofiore the "value theory of labor"[54]), but, for the purposes of this work, there is one feature which stands out as important for the argument that follows: the reversibility of the capitalist value-form as money. Capitalist production begins with an initial act of expenditure where money is converted into commodified labor power, commodified material inputs and invested as fixed capital in means of production (which at one degree removed is a combination of expended labor power and transformed material inputs). Once an output is produced through the material transformation of the

100 (July–August 2016): 99–117, https://newleftreview.org/issues/ii100/articles/nancy-fraser-contradictions-of-capital-and-care.
53.   See Bhattacharyya, *Rethinking Racial Capitalism*.
54.   Riccardo Bellofiore, "The Multiple Meanings of Marx's Value Theory," *Monthly Review* 69(11) (2018), https://monthlyreview.org/2018/04/01/the-multiple-meanings-of-marxs-value-theory/.

inputs by effort and work of labor mediated by fixed capital, it takes the form of a commodity to be sold and consumed. The conditions of consumption of the final output depend on the degree of subsumption of the reproductive process, and this will determine the use and end-of-use of the commodity, but this moment of consumption is not, from a capitalist perspective, the finality of production.[55]

From a capitalist standpoint, the finality of production is the metamorphosis of the valued output from its commodity form back into a money form, ready to be expended again. Not only is the initial expenditure of money needed to launch the productive process recovered but added to this amount is a surplus that also has a money form. We will discuss further the origins of this surplus; the point here is that it also has a value-form and is accumulated as money. Capitalist production presents itself as a circular process and the metamorphoses of capital seem to have the property of reversibility. Money as capital, though expended and subject to a series of metamorphoses, reverts back to its initial money form unscathed and even expanded as a mass at the end of its process. This reversibility of the capitalist value-form strongly contrasts with the thermodynamic irreversibility of the underlying material throughput process studied from a metabolic perspective. Furthermore, the monetary circuit of capitalist production and consumption also obscures other economic relations essential to capitalism from a metabolic perspective. Before production, there is a prior economic relation of extraction that ensures that capital will find commodified material inputs ready to be bought and transformed. Reducing the metabolic process of appropriation of this matter to a process of production obscures the socio-ecological particularities of extractive relations. The same can be said of the moment that follows the capitalist realization of value. If, for the capitalist, value as money flows neatly back to his coffers, from a metabolic perspective the outputs trajectory is still ongoing, from commodity in the market, to use, to disposal and waste, the output is subject to a series of linear and irreversible—but socially (and capitalistically) conditioned—material metamorphosis that does not end with matter retrieving its initial form and potentialities. This disjuncture between the valued output and its surplus as capital, and the material throughput is a core theoretical

---

55.   Abstraction is made of intermediary as well as investment goods and services to focus on final goods.

element of the perspective outlined in this book as a social ecology of capital. Much more could be said on the topic of value; some problems will be taken up in later chapters, but the reader expecting a novel theory in this field or an in-depth discussion of the classical theory of value and its limits in light of current developments by feminist, ecological and post-colonial critiques of capitalism will be disappointed.[56] This would be a project onto itself and would probably imply many volumes of study. Given that much can be understood and analyzed by examining how prices are formed in an advanced capitalist economy through monopolistic practices and disruptive cycles of competition, we will focus on these monetary aspects of the value-form, leaving to one side the thorny but highly metaphysical question of the nature and inner workings of the value-substance presumed to exert a causality on prices.[57]

---

56. Some recent and interesting interventions on this question are to be found in: Elke Pirgmaier, "The Value of Value Theory for Ecological Economics," *Ecological Economics* 179 (2021): 106790, https://doi.org/10.1016/j.ecolecon.2020.106790; Alf Hornborg, "Why Ecological Economics Should Not Adopt Marxian Value Theory," *Ecological Economics* 193 (2022): 107334, https://doi.org/10.1016/j.ecolecon.2021.107334; John Bellamy Foster and Paul Burkett, "Value Isn't Everything," *Monthly Review* 70(6) (November 2018), https://monthlyreview.org/2018/11/01/value-isnt-everything/; Giorgos Kallis and Erik Swyngedouw, "Do Bees Produce Value? A Conversation Between an Ecological Economist and a Marxist Geographer," *Capitalism Nature Socialism* 29(3) (2018): 36–50, https://doi.org/10.1080/10455752.2017.1315830; and Jason W. Moore, "The Value of Everything? Work, Capital, and Historical Nature in the Capitalist World-Ecology," *Review* 37(3–4) (2014): 245–292.
57. On the question of value, we have adopted an analytical strategy similar to the one employed by Paul A. Baran and Paul M. Sweezy in their classical work *Monopoly Capital: An Essay on the American Economic and Social Order*. New York: Monthly Review Press, 1966. It is also an approach shared by economists following the perspective opened up by Kalecki, both have profoundly marked the understanding of capitalist accumulation dynamics that led to this book. Finally, a discussion of value today cannot in my mind start immediately with Marx, it must start with the meta-economic question of value as a social form and particular institution. I would tend, in this light, to define value as a mediation that works by creating boundaries, separations and frontiers inside the social process of production. Value institutes boundaries and legitimates separations between worth and unworth, in capitalist economies this boundary is built through the productive–unproductive binary as argued by the Bielefeld feminists. On this, see the excellent paper by Adelheid Biesecker and Sabine Hofmeister, "Focus: (Re)productivity: Sustainable Relations Both Between Society and Nature and Between the Genders," *Ecological Economics* 69(8) (2010): 1703–1711. One would have to start with this problem: in what context and in what manner is a value boundary institutionalized? In this light, value is always also devaluation.

ACCUMULATION AS REGIME

With value, the last core concept that needs a prior definition in this work is that of accumulation. Accumulation of capital is both the result of the workings of the production and consumption of the valued output, the recovery of its monetary form as an economic surplus and it is also the pre-condition of capitalist reproduction. Capital investment, and capitalist production in general, is possible because capital as money has been accumulated in the reversible economic circuit of value. Accumulation is an imperative faced by each and every capitalist, with its grow or die corollary imposed on producers, coercing them to invest in the expansion of the economic process of capital, and thus driving and directing social metabolism. Accumulation, as a regime, is a conceptual tool that captures this expanded reproduction of capital as a totality and as a societal trajectory. It models the macroeconomic structure of a capitalist economy as system of social relations mediated by monetized production, investment and consumption practices.

The Regulation school of critical political economy has offered a powerful set of explanatory tools to understand these relations and how they come together as different accumulation regimes.[58] These models can be formalized and given a mathematical expression, or they can be constructed through institutional analysis that defines narratively the constitutive social relations and practices of these formations. This latter methodological option is the approach used in this work. According to Regulation Theory, accumulation regimes emerge through a conflictual and contingent process of institutionalization of specific economic relations of production, consumption and of income distribution between classes which ensure the compatibility between the development of productive capacity and the evolution of demand, structuring the conflictual relations between capital and labor. This leads to an investment pattern that stabilizes the accumulation process of the economy as a whole around a specific growth trajectory.[59]

---

58. For a classical overview, see Robert Jessop, "Regulation Theory in Retrospect and Prospect," *Economy and Society* 19(2) (1990): 153–216; and "Twenty Years of the (Parisian) Regulation Approach: The Paradox of Success and Failure at Home and Abroad," *New Political Economy* 2(3) (1997): 499–522.

59. For an in-depth discussion, see Pineault, "The Ghosts of Progress."

In the recent history of critical political economy, there have been a large diversity of typologies of accumulation regimes that have distinguished different periods, regions and countries according to a variety of logics of economic reproduction.[60] The archetypical accumulation regime is "Fordism" proposed by Michel Aglietta in his seminal *A Theory of Capitalist Regulation*, originally published in French in 1976. He sought to explain the socio-political and socio-economic stability and strong growth of advanced capitalist societies during the post-war era and the reasons for the subsequent breakdown of this structure in the mid-1970s. His empirical basis was the specific trajectory of the American capitalist economy from the mid-nineteenth century onwards and his theoretical toolkit was a combination of Marxian economics, post-Keynesian monetary theory and institutionalist economics, as well as Althusserian epistemology. The result was a theory of Fordism, which in various forms both as a theoretical framework and as a narrative was rapidly adopted by critical political economists in a wide range of social sciences from the 1980s onwards. Regulation Theory proposed a golden age model of growth during which the wage relation articulated demand and output supply by tying workers' real income to productivity gains. In this accumulation regime, production levels and investments in new productive capacity were in a sense pre-validated by the nature of the wage relation, setting the stage for three decades of virtuous growth and quasi full employment for "breadwinning" (white) males in the advanced capitalist core of North America and Western Europe. The breakdown of this wage relation as a mode of regulation of accumulation during the 1970s has been explained in many contradictory ways. Even if all agree that we have moved away from "Fordism" in the advanced capitalist core, there is no agreement on how to characterize the regime, or regimes, that have come after.

This book proposes a different perspective on the trajectory of advanced capitalism. Taking a step back from the various historical and local typologies of accumulation regimes used to characterize the tra-

---

60. For a recent analysis of the global trajectory of capitalist accumulation in a metabolic perspective from the Vienna school of social ecology, see Christoph Görg et al., "Scrutinizing the Great Acceleration: The Anthropocene and its Analytic Challenges for Social–Ecological Transformations," *Anthropocene Review* 7(1) (2019): 42–61, https://doi.org/10.1177/2053019619895034. *A Social Ecology of Capital* can be read as contribution to the research program outlined in this paper.

jectories of a variety of capitalisms during the twentieth and into the twenty-first century, we are interested in the permanent and structural features of accumulation throughout the last 100 years. Where Regulation Theory saw an economically virtuous and socially progressive coupling of productivity and real wage growth as an outcome of class struggle and social compromise, a social ecology of capital rather understands the Fordist compact and what comes after as part of an accumulation regime regulated by an enduring and structural constraint of economic surplus absorption and its expansive metabolism. What do we mean by a regime structured by constraint of economic surplus absorption? Following the Monopoly Capital school, we can distinguish an accumulation regime faced with an economic surplus production constraint from a regime faced with the problem of economic surplus absorption constraint. In the former situation, which roughly corresponds to the capitalist dynamics that confronted Marx in the nineteenth century, capitalist development is primarily driven and limited by the "valorization" moment of accumulation. A surplus absorption constrained regime sees the locus of contradiction and limits to development shift to the "realization" moment of accumulation.[61]

In most historical formations of economic exploitation subordinate classes are mobilized by the dominant classes in a process of surplus extraction, a surplus appropriated, accumulated and consumed by the dominant groups in forms necessary for the reproduction of their social power and of the overall structure of exploitation. We can define advanced capitalism as a social formation where added to these relations of economic exploitation is the further imperative that a significant segment of the subordinate classes absorb, consume and waste the very surplus they produce. Of course, this surplus is not directly absorbed by its producers, that would resemble some form of socialist economy, it is absorbed rather through an economic process that reproduces the organizational

61. This is a rather classical distinction; it was discussed in the 1940s in Paul Sweezy's *The Theory of Capitalist Development: Principles of Marxian Political Economy* (New York: Oxford University Press, 1942), as well as in the 1950s in Paul Baran's *The Political Economy of Growth* (New York: Monthly Review Press, 1957) and also forms the basis for their joint development of Monopoly Capital theory in the 1960s that came together in their seminal *Monopoly Capital*, it is also present in the writings of prominent post-Keynesian economist Joan Robinson. See Paul A. Baran and Paul M. Sweezy, *Monopoly Capital: An Essay on the American Economic and Social Order*. New York: Monthly Review Press, 1966.

capacity of capital to generate, extract and manage the growing surplus. Surplus absorption is very unequally spread across subordinated classes and groups. Some are privileged individual surplus absorbers with large ecological footprints, others, underprivileged—marginalized, racialized and colonized—absorb the surplus in the form of cheap and shanty use-values and toxic and/or unhealthy food and beverages.[62] And in between there exists a plethora of situations. Finally, surplus absorption is also a collective affair, embedded in our public infrastructures and services. If this surplus is not adequately absorbed then this accumulation regime is faced with a crisis of "over-accumulation," a significant proportion of the output will not be consumed, idled fixed capital will be devalorized and new investments will be cancelled for lack of profitable outlets.

The stability and viability of such an accumulation regime then, the reproduction of the overall structure of exploitation, rests on the capacity to mobilize the social activity of subordinate classes not solely as surplus producers but also and crucially as surplus absorbers in what we can call, following the seminal work of Allan Schnaiberg, a treadmill of "overproduction validated by overconsumption."[63] Overproduction has always been a problem for capitalists. In advanced capitalism, this contradiction is displaced by the organization on a massive scale of what is decried by environmentalists and growth critique as overconsumption. Overconsumption, as understood in our work, is not what results from gluttonous, gullible or narrowly materialistic spendthrift subjects alienated by the "sales effort" of advanced capitalism, subjects who should either shop less or buy better—more ecological and ethical—commodities and services. This moral conception often present in ecological critiques of consumption misses the deeper social determinations that actually drive the process. Overconsumption is a structural feature tied to the dialectic of subsumption of social reproduction by capital that we have previously outlined. As the process of subsumption shifts from formal to real, we can speak of overconsumption when the nature of the material objects on which life affirmation and subsistence comes to depend, their churn rate, the abstract energy, organic and inorganic matter embedded in their pro-

---

62. An excellent discussion of this dynamic illustrated by the rise of ramen soup consumption among working classes in Asia can be found in Max Haiven, *Palm Oil: The Grease of Empire*. London: Pluto Press, 2022.
63. Allan Schnaiberg, *The Environment: From Surplus to Scarcity*. New York: Oxford University Press, 1980.

duction and circulation, all act as surplus absorption mechanisms. Based on the work of Baran and Sweezy, John Bellamy Foster has proposed the concept of "capitalistically determined use-value" to describe this central mechanism of surplus absorption in advanced capitalism, a concept which we have mobilized in this work, in particular to analyze the mode of existence of commodified artifacts that structure daily life and social practices in contemporary capitalist societies.[64] Displacement becomes the new central growth driving mechanism in capitalism, it redefines both extensive and intensive forms of accumulation as well as the boundaries between the monetized sphere of the economy and the sphere of reproduction organized around non-monetized forms of provisioning and care. The agents of this displacement, meaning the forms of capital that on one hand are constrained to overproduce and on the other hand organize the subsumption of social reproduction as overconsumption, are large organizationally integrated monopolistic corporations.

Before exploring, in a critical manner, the socio-ecological logic of accumulation that results from the practices of these entities, we will plunge into the peculiar materiality of the economic process of capitalist society. This journey into the world of mass flows and accumulations of matter will bring us beyond the veneer of capitalist commodities and the shiny artifacts designed to excite the senses and distract the mind. We will uncover a materiality of capitalist metabolism that is dreary, dull and grim, like the asphalt, crushed stone, cement and concrete that shapes most of the lifeworld around us, like the smoke billowed by the combustion of the coal, gas and oil that powers the machines that free (some of) us from toil, multiply and extend our corporeal capacities, like the monocultures of soya, corn and palm trees that generate the biomass that feeds our bodies or those bodies we slaughter and eat. After having studied the mass flows and accumulations of matter that characterize capitalism today, we will delineate the structure and logic of capitalist metabolism as a socio-ecological regime. Capitalist economies and societies are bounded in their development by the constraints and potentialities of their metabolic bases; the study of these bases as "metabolic regimes" forms the central chapters of this work. Finally, in the closing chapters,

---

64. John Bellamy Foster, "The Ecology of Marxian Political Economy," *Monthly Review* 63(4) (September 2011): 1–16, https://monthlyreview.org/2011/09/01/the-ecology-of-marxian-political-economy/.

we will return to the study of advanced capitalist accumulation dynamics which takes into account its biophysical foundation and socio-ecological determinations and consequences. We hope to convince the reader that this approach provides the necessary conceptual tools for a social ecology of capitalist societies that is both consistent and rigorous as well as politically relevant as critical theory and useful to socio-ecological movements contesting the material trajectory of our times.

1

The Material Flow

Social wealth in capitalist societies appears as a continuous and over-flowing output of goods and services. From global commodity chains to distribution hubs, to points of collective or individualized consumption, monetary exchange governs and regulates the production and consumption of this valued output. Capital and labor struggle over its conditions of production and distribution, governments intervene as stewards of its expansion, GDP measures its growth. In a capitalist society, the valued output is considered the material basis of social life, of subsistence and societal reproduction. Ideally, the valued output should guarantee not only a meek subsistence, but flourishing societies and a good life for all. Growing the output, either as a mass of exchange or of use-values, has been the primary means to achieve these goals in modern societies. Systems of political economy offer varying and contrasted views on how to organize capital, labor and state relations to best achieve this growth and distribute rights to the use and consumption of the expanding valued output according to different conceptions of justice.

The object of social ecology, and of this inquiry, is the material throughput out of which this output is drawn, on which it is based and the ecological relations that develop along its flow. If the valued output presents itself as a "vast collection of commodities"—capital goods, consumer goods, services, buildings and infrastructures—the throughput is the mass flow of energy and matter that a society mobilizes, transforms and dissipates in its economic process in order to produce, consume and use this valued output. The throughput is thus a much broader category and reality than the economic output.[1] Encompassing a wide and diverse

---

1. Ecological economist Herman Daly, in his textbook *Steady-State Economics*, offers this definition of the throughput: "the entropic physical flow of matter-energy from natures sources, through the human economy, and back to natures sinks"; Herman E. Daly, *Steady-State Economics*, 2nd ed. with New Essays. Washington, DC: Island

ensemble of materialities, it determines both the social relations to nature and the ecological contradictions of capitalist development. Yet, many aspects of this material flow remain hidden or invisible in everyday productive, consumptive and reproductive practices and representations. For example, in the last half century, it has been realized that economic activities generate carbon emissions that are destabilizing the Earth's climate, yet visibilizing the material flow of carbon or methane has proven challenging for modern capitalist societies. And this is but one of the many crucial material flows entangled in their economic process.

The valued output's circulation is bounded by social relations of production and consumption; this is the usual mode of representation of the economic process in modern capitalist society: ecological relations and natural processes appear entirely external to these economic relations. Bringing them to the fore requires a shift of focus from the metrics and categories of the valued output to new categories able to express the materiality of the throughput and the mediation of the economic process by the biophysical determinations of the material flow. We do not need to invent the categories and metrics able to represent the throughput; the recent development of material flow analysis and material flow national accounts provides us with the necessary conceptual tools, vocabulary and data.[2] It is from inside this perspective that we will begin our inquiry into the social ecology of capital by exploring more deeply the structure, substance and dynamics of the throughput, as well as its accumulation as material stocks in the form of the inert artifacts that saturate capitalist worlds.

Press, 1991, 36. The throughput, according to Daly, is the "ultimate biophysical cost" of economic production and consumption, measured not in monetary value, but in entropy and ecosystem service loss; Daly, *Steady-State Economics*, 37. Though he didn't use the category nominally, the throughput concept was pioneered by Georgescu-Roegen in the 1970s as he explored in *The Entropy Law and the Economic Process* (Cambridge, MA: Harvard University Press, 1971), as well as in his essay on Energy myths, the economy's structure and dynamics as a system of biophysical processes subject to the laws of thermodynamics. See also Nicholas Georgescu-Roegen, "Energy and Economic Myths," *Southern Economic Journal* 41(3) (January 1975): 347–381.

2. Most of our data and categories will be drawn from the United Nations Environment Programme (UNEP) international resource panel global material flows database, at: www.resourcepanel.org/global-material-flows-database. More refined data and concepts on material stocks draws on work by the Vienna Institute of Social Ecology to which this work is highly indebted, https://boku.ac.at/en/wiso/sec.

A LINEAR THROUGHPUT

From the biophysical perspective of social ecology, the economic process takes the form of a continuous mass flow of matter and energy extracted from natural environments (ecosystems, geological formations, the atmosphere, the oceans), transformed and then dissipated by social relations of production, consumption and use. This throughput flow is necessary for the continued existence of capitalist society. Social relations do not in and of themselves act on matter; they govern the material flow through the mediation of social practices. Labor is one ensemble of such practices, and it was the focus of Marx's metabolic analysis in *Capital*, but so are provisioning and care, reproductive work as well as expressive and symbolic practices in general mediated by culture. Taken as a whole, it can be said that capitalist society governs reflexively the throughput flow through its economic process and the social relations and institutions on which it is founded. This social reflexivity is largely, but not exclusively, determined by the capitalist imperative of accumulation.

A simple graphical illustration of the material throughput of capitalist society is shown in Figure 1.1. In this linear process, energy and matter extracted from natural sources (and resulting from ecological and geological processes) are given social form and function, put to work (in a physical sense), used (in a social sense) and, as waste (in a social sense), dissipated (in a physical sense) into natural sinks. The throughputs structure is built around a nature/society boundary with sources and sinks as the interfaces between the economic process and ecological as well as biogeochemical processes.[3] The throughput flow includes all matter that is extracted by the economic process of modern societies, whether the element finds its way into the valued output or not, this includes processing wastes and commercial wastes such as unsold goods. The flow ends when this material mass is sunk in various physical states—be they

---

3. As we will argue in Chapter 2, by "nature" in this work, we refer to an order of causality distinct and autonomous from social causality organized around symbolic and institutional structures. This definition of nature is processual, nature is not "out there" it is a dialectical other of social processes. An apt representation in common sense would be what we signify when we use the expression "nature calls" and we could oppose this prosaic mode of representing nature with the much more romanticized and problematic signifier found in the expression "the call of the wild," nature as wilderness, pristine and feral.

solid, gaseous or liquid—into ecosystems and absorbed in biogeochemical cycles with varying capacities to reduce this waste.[4] Social ecology considers source and sink interfaces not as closed boundaries but rather as structures of intermediation and interpenetration of social and biophysical processes and causalities.[5]

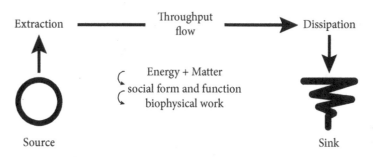

Figure 1.1   Basic throughput structure
Source: Author.

As throughput, extracted matter *flows* as a mass *through* society in a dual manner:

1. its social form is successively regulated and governed by different moments of the economic process (social relations of production, consumption, use and waste) and this brings about a series of changes in the biophysical form of the throughput. Flow then refers to the change of form and function of matter, its successive biophysical transformations informed and regulated by social relations and practices;

2. the flow is also a spatial process, matter is purposefully moved and continuously put into physical circulation by the economic process[6]

---

4.   Any circularity internal to the economic process or society, such as recycling and industrial ecology schemes are part of the throughput process inasmuch as they imply eventually new inputs of matter and energy and generate waste. We will return to this question later.
5.   Marina Fischer-Kowalski and Helmut Haberl, "Tons, Joules, and Money: Modes of Production and Their Sustainability Problems," *Society and Natural Resources* 10(1) (1997): 61–85, https://doi.org/10.1080/08941929709381009.
6.   Other social processes contribute and regulate mass material flows in modern societies, in particular state practices such as war and the organization of territoriality as well as infrastructure tied to social services and policing of societies. Our focus

and, in advanced capitalism these flows have taken on a massive scale as will be seen.

Figure 1.2 shows the linear throughput using the language of modern material flow accounting. In this schema, the inflow from nature to society is known as "material extraction," the outflow is the "processed output" and between the outflow and inflow is the socio-metabolic process of "material consumption."[7] Together, they circumscribe the substance of the throughput as an aggregated mass of flowing matter. Mass is also the mode of representation adopted by material flow accounting which measures material extraction, material consumption and processed output in tonnes of aggregated matter.

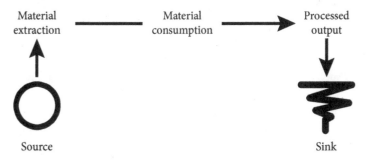

Figure 1.2   Throughput according to material flow accounting
Source: Author.

The scale of a capitalist economy can be measured as the aggregate throughput in tonnes of material consumption, which is also a means of expressing and measuring capitalist growth. The larger this material flow, the greater the environmental impact at both ends of the economic

---

in this work being the social ecology of capital, these flows and the practices they intermediate will be examined inasmuch as they are part of the economic process of capital accumulation. This attribution is purely methodological and does not in any way imply the primacy of the economic sphere over others.

7.   The above definitions concern a closed economy without imports and exports. They apply for example at the global level, country level analysis implies calculating imported and exported raw materials as well as material flows embedded in imported finished and semi-finished products as well as in services, this is captured by the category "raw material consumption." For an overview, the reader can go to the website "materialflows.net" and generate global as well as country specific data on throughput flows.

process. The greater the aggregated throughput, the greater material extraction and the larger the processed output. Scale of the throughput will indicate how, at the point of extraction and the point of dissipation, sources and sinks will be forced, how ecosystems as well as the biogeochemical cycles that perform or sustain these source and sink functions will be perturbed and will breakdown or change in a non-linear fashion. Examples of forced sources are marine ecosystems incapable of adapting to the mass extraction of marine life by industrial capitalist fisheries, collapse of biodiversity in forest ecosystems exploited by logging and pulp and paper corporations, collapse of soil ecosystems exploited by intensive industrial agriculture, on top of depletion of accessible abiotic resources such as metals, minerals and fossil fuels. To this must be added the forcing of large sinks such as the carbon cycle, the nitrogen and phosphorous cycles, with dire consequences for human and non-humans alike as these forcings provoke ecological feedback loops through destabilized ecosystems. Of course, very small quantities of highly reactive and toxic matter such as pesticides or nuclear waste have important environmental effects, but mass flows implying both mass extraction and mass waste, as well as mass accumulation of material stocks in various forms, determine in a fundamental way social relations to nature in capitalism, profoundly transforming ecosystems and biogeochemical earth processes at a global scale.

Figure 1.3 gives a first representation of this biophysical scale of the global economic process over the last half century by tracing the growth of the aggregated throughput from 1970 to 2017 in billion tonnes of extracted matter per year. During this period, extraction and thus global material consumption,[8] grew by a factor of 3.4, from 27 gigatonnes (billion tonnes) per annum to a little over 92 gigatonnes (billion tonnes) per annum in 2017.[9] To put the scale of the global throughput into perspective, biomass flows originating from the net primary production of all the Earth's terrestrial ecosystems at the beginning of the twenty-first century

8. At the global level, domestic extraction = material consumption, whereas at the country level, material consumption includes imported extracted materials and excludes exported raw materials.
9. The data used in this chapter is mainly drawn from the "Global Material Flows Database," from UN International Resources Panel (2018), www.resourcepanel.org/global-material-flows-database, on which the visualization tools of "materialflows.net" are based.

has been estimated at 118 gigatonnes (Gt).[10] The flow of matter extracted and transformed by capitalist societies—92Gt—thus approaches in scale global terrestrial biomass flows 118Gt, the totality of matter organized through photosynthesis on land and available for the flourishing of all terrestrial living beings, humanity included.

Figure 1.3 also shows that part of the throughput which circulates through global trade as exported raw materials, an amount that represented 2.6 Gt in 1970 and has grown to 11.5 Gt in 2017. International flows of matter have grown by a factor of 4.4 during this period, much faster than the overall extracted throughput.

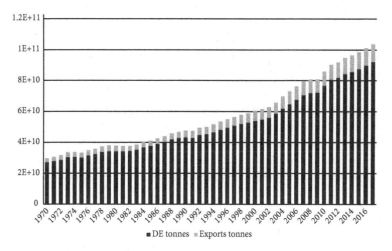

Figure 1.3   Global material flows, 1970–2017

Source: "Global Material Flows Database," UN International Resources Panel (2018), www.resourcepanel.org/global-material-flows-database.

Though useful as a representation of the planetary scale of extraction, aggregating material flows at the global level hides wide regional discrepancies between core and periphery, between emerging and mature capitalist societies. Figure 1.4 presents annual material consumption per capita for various regions of the globe and captures the material inequal-

---

10. Fridolin Krausmann, Karl-Heinz Erb, Simone Gingrich, Christian Lauk and Helmut Haberl, "Global Patterns of Socioeconomic Biomass Flows in the Year 2000: A Comprehensive Assessment of Supply, Consumption and Constraints," *Ecological Economics* 65(3) (2008): 471–487, https://doi.org/10.1016/j.ecolecon.2007.07.012.

ity between societies as well as processes of convergence. Hovering since the 1970s between 20 and 30 tonnes per capita per year (average 27), North Americans were, in recent history, by far the largest consumers of extracted material flows, followed by Europeans with an average consumption at 14 tonnes. Both have since been surpassed by the ascendance of China up from 2.6 tonnes per capita in 1970 to 23.6 tonnes in 2015; Latin America has grown its per capita material consumption to 12.9 tonnes in 2015, a level that approaches that of Europeans.

Another important empirical finding in Figure 1.4 is the high sensitivity of the throughput flow to economic cycles in the advanced capitalist core. North America and Europe saw their material flows drop sharply in the wake of the 2008 financial crisis, the collapse of material consumption in the United States is particularly impressive plunging by almost a third, from 30 tonnes at the height of the housing boom in 2006 to 21 tonnes in 2015. Similar variations can be observed during past economic cycles which show up as troughs of material consumption after the recessions that hit these economies in the early 1980s and 1990s. This leads to the important observation that economic activity and material extraction and consumption in the advanced capitalist core are strongly coupled.

The metric of material consumption measures all inflows of matter into a given economy whether extracted domestically or flowing in as imports.

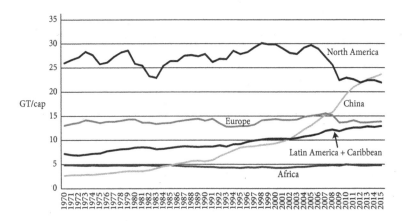

Figure 1.4   Material consumption by world region, Gt per capita, 1970–2015
Source: "Global Material Flows Database," UN International Resources Panel (2018), www. resourcepanel.org/global-material-flows-database.

What it does not capture are those material flows which are needed to generate imported goods but that do not enter into their final composition. So material consumption will capture the matter in the smartphones shipped from China to the USA, the aluminum, plastics, silicon, lithium and critical metals such as dysprosium,[11] but not the coal that was burnt to generate the electricity that powered the machines on the smartphone assembly lines.[12] A more complete representation of the material footprint of a society is captured by measuring its "raw material consumption" which accounts for these indirect flows; this is done by calculating "raw material equivalents" of imports into a given society's throughput.[13] For example, in 2017, China exported to the world 404 million tonnes of matter (0.4 Gt), but their raw material equivalent was 9.2 billion tonnes (9.2 Gt). Put another way, the throughput extracted and transformed to produce Chinese exports was 23 times the size of the exported output that left the docks. The throughput to output ratio can also be applied to imports. The mass of the output produced the world over and imported into the United States in 2015 was 0.9 Gt, while the throughput behind this output was 5.9 Gt, close to six times larger than the apparent output. The trend over time is for this ratio to grow as economies have become more globalized. In 1990, the ratio of throughput to output of the imports absorbed by North America was 2.7 to 1; it doubled in the last 27 years. For Europe, the value of this ratio is not as high and its growth is not as impressive, but still, in 1990 it was 2.1 and in 2017 it had grown to 3.3. This illustrates a theoretical principle presented at the beginning of this chapter: the material flows that come together as the throughput are much larger than the apparent material output of the economic process. Hidden behind each kilogram of commodities imported from China is a flow of

---

11.   Julie Michelle Klinger, *Rare Earth Frontiers: From Terrestrial Subsoils to Lunar Landscapes*. Ithaca, NY: Cornell University Press, 2017. www.jstor.org/stable/10.7591/j. ctt1wodd6d.

12.   Nor does it capture the biomass needed to produce the ramen noodle packs that sustained the laborers working on the smartphone assembly lines (basically palm oil and wheat) for that matter. Material flow accounts do not consider these flows that sustain labor. On ramen, see Max Haiven, *Palm Oil: The Grease of Empire*. London: Pluto Press, 2022.

13.   For an exploration of the methods and a discussion of the controversies implied in the calculation of raw material equivalents of imports and exports, see Anke Schaffartzik, Dominik Wiedenhofer and Nina Eisenmenger, "Raw Material Equivalents: The Challenges of Accounting for Sustainability in a Globalized World," *Sustainability* (Switzerland) 7(5) (2015): 5345–5370, https://doi.org/10.3390/su7055345.

23kg of extracted and transformed matter. And behind each kilogram of commodities imported by the United States of America in 2017, one finds 7.3kg of extracted and transformed matter, in the UK, the throughput to output ratio of imports is 5.3, in Germany, it stands near the European average of 3, while Germany's exports have a ratio of 2.3 to 1.

When "raw material equivalents" of imports are used to correct the measurement of domestic material consumption, one obtains the material footprint of a society, the quantity of tonnes of matter mobilized by its economic process, or its real throughput. Presented on a per capita basis, inequalities between the advanced core and peripheries become sharper. Figure 1.5 shows this footprint on a per capita, per year basis, for the same global regions but for a shorter time span, from 1990 to 2015. In 2015, the material consumption, on throughput basis, of North American is 32.5 tonnes per capita, in Europe it stands at 21 tonnes per capita, in China this number is at 19.9 tonnes per capita, while Africa and India, respectively at 3.1 and 4.4 are well below the world average of 12, which is the size of per capita throughput flows in Latin America and the Caribbean.

This wider measure of material flows also dispels the illusion that the advanced capitalist core has seen its material consumption stagnate or fall in the last decades as so-called "dematerialized" services have grown

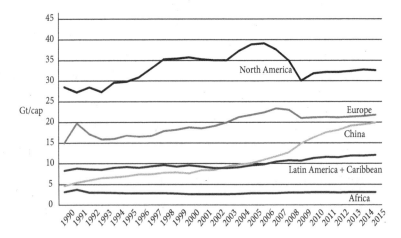

Figure 1.5 Material footprint per capita, 1990–2015

Source: "Global Material Flows Database," UN International Resources Panel (2018), www.resourcepanel.org/global-material-flows-database.

as a share of the valued output, the so-called decoupling hypothesis.[14] On the contrary, over the whole period, consumption of extracted matter has grown in Europe and North America roughly on par with the growth of global per capita raw material consumption. Again, this growth was impacted by economic cycles, but the variations are not as sharp, for example, in the case of North America, the post-2008 crisis contraction of material flows does not dip below the 30-tonne floor crossed in the mid-1990s. Actually, only Africa has seen a net drop in its per capita raw material consumption over this period. Finally, the footprint analysis shows even greater inequality than the prior measurement of material flows per capita. North Americans in 2017 consumed almost three times the world average, Europeans twice.[15]

FROM STRUCTURE TO SUBSTANCE

Measuring the throughput as an undifferentiated mass of matter captures in the abstract the metabolic scale of an economy, yet it ignores the diverse and variegated flows of material elements that capitalist societies extract, transform and dissipate as waste. The material composition of the throughput can be broken down and characterized in various ways. From a purely biophysical perspective, a description at the molecular level would make sense; this is the method used in greenhouse gas accounting. From the perspective of social ecology, the qualitative characteristics of the throughput are determined by the different social relations that mediate its flow.

At the point of extraction, material flow accounting breaks down the throughput into four broad categories; these correspond to the biophysical forms that flows take on for society as appropriated raw materials: fossil fuels, biomass, metals and non-metallic minerals. For the year 2017, the global material throughput was composed of 24 Gt of biomass, 15 Gt of fossil fuels, 9 Gt of metals and 44 Gt of non-metal minerals, (primarily

---

14. Timothée Parrique et al., "Decoupling Debunked: Evidence and Arguments Against Green Growth as a sole strategy for Sustainability," European Environmental Bureau, 2019, at: eeb.org/library/decoupling-debunked.

15. And these metrics do not include intra-societal material inequality, which is tied to socio-economic inequality.

sand, gravel as well as limestone, but also phosphates and potassium). In terms of shear mass, this latter category, "non-metal minerals," dominates the throughput flow, accounting for 48 percent of matter globally extracted.

Figure 1.6 presents anew the growth of the throughput flow from 1970 to 2017 based on these four generic categories. As the graph shows, though the mass flows of all material categories have grown, metals and non-metal minerals have significantly higher growth rates than biomass and fossil fuels; these materials are typically accumulated as stocks, whereas biomass and fossil fuels typically are flow-through materials which are rapidly dissipated.

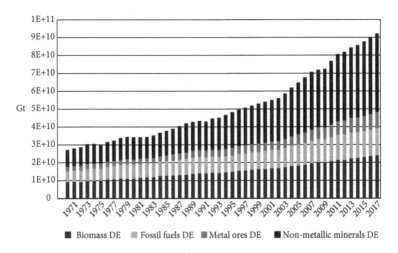

Figure 1.6   Domestic extraction of world by material group, 1970–2017
Source: "Global Material Flows Database," UN International Resources Panel (2018), www.resourcepanel.org/global-material-flows-database.

We can further disaggregate the above global material flows using finer grained data of extracted matter as shown for the year 2017 in Figure 1.7. With these 13 categories, we have a more precise representation of the material substances that modern capitalist societies extract and appropriate as raw materials to reproduce their metabolism. (The entries in Figure 1.7 are color coded according to the four broad categories presented in Figure 1.6). Non-metallic minerals for construction and infrastructure development, basically, sand, gravel and limestone used to make cement, dominate by a wide margin the metabolic flow of modern societies, making up 46 percent of its mass. If we exclude these bulky materials, the other main components of the throughput from crops to minerals used in agriculture and industry represent a yearly flow from 9.5 to a 0.8Gt of matter.

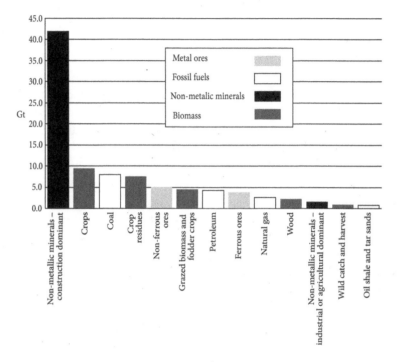

Figure 1.7   Global material flows (gt), 2017

Source: "Global Material Flows Database," UN International Resources Panel (2018), www.resourcepanel.org/global-material-flows-database.

The categories of raw extraction do not explain the flow of matter through society, only the form they take on at the point of extraction, typically represented as raw materials and "natural resources." As these variegated materials flow into social relations of production and consumption, they are transformed and take on new guises that correspond to the functional characteristics they acquire as "use-values" to borrow a category from classical political economy. Material flow analysis will, for example, distinguish matter that is transformed and circulates as food, as feed, as energy carriers, and materials that are used dissipatedly,[16] from those that are used to build up stocks of artifacts in manufacturing or construction. These functional categories are essential to trace the flow of matter through social relations of production and consumption, but they do not explain why a given form of matter, such as corn, for example, will flow either as feed, as food or as (inefficient) fuel. As remarked by Marx in *Capital*, it would be an analytical mistake to suppose that in a capitalist society functionality is defined unilaterally by the chemical, biological or physical potentiality of a material element, or that the use-value of a specific material form corresponds to a universal and transcendental social need such as the need for fuel, food, fodder or feed and fiber. In a capitalist economy, it is the valorization and accumulation imperatives that define functionality and that mediate the biophysical transformation and circulation of the throughput. In the terminology of Marxian political economy, use-value is subsumed by exchange-value (and this subsumption is real, not merely formal), a defining feature of advanced capitalism.[17]

The last stretch of the linear flow sees matter moving from use to waste, the economic and social relations that govern these practices also impact the qualitative nature of the throughput. Having worked as use-values in the productive sphere, having been valorized as exchange values, used in the consumptive sphere, matter will eventually take on various waste forms: material processing wastes, ashes, carcasses, excrements, solid end of life wastes, gaseous emissions, leachate. Material flow accounting categorizes as "domestic processed output" the ultimate form taken on by the throughput when it reaches what we have called the point of dissipation where it is absorbed by biophysical sinks. Just as functionality in a capitalist society is overdetermined and shaped by the imperatives of valorization and capital accumulation, so is the flow of matter into the category of waste. The frontier between that part of the throughput that belongs to the valued output, and that part that becomes waste is a

---

16. This refers to matter that performs biophysical work through its controlled dissipation in the environment, either for its chemical properties as a reactant, such as fertilizers or for its physical properties such as calcium salts, sand and gravel on icy roads and sidewalks.

17. On this, see John Bellamy Foster, "The Ecology of Marxian Political Economy," *Monthly Review* 63(4) (September 2011), https://monthlyreview.org/2011/09/01/the-ecology-of-marxian-political-economy/.

socio-economic construct that has more to do with the imperatives of capital accumulation than with purely technological obsolescence and biophysical degradation.

To sum up what we have learnt concerning the structure and substance of the throughput thus far: it appears as a flowing mass from source to sink that can be aggregated as an abstract quantum of extracted matter. This quantum captures the metabolic scale of an economy and its evolution over time expresses capitalist growth as a material phenomenon. Yet, societies do not experience the throughput as an abstract mass flow. They rather experience the flow of a differentiated mass of matter formed by social relations of extraction, production, consumption and dissipation. The composition of the throughput determines in great part the ecological impact and biophysical entanglements of the material flows that capitalist societies have come to depend on.

Table 1.1 Metamorphosis of the throughput

Extraction	*Raw material consumption*	*Processed output*
Raw materials → Extractive form	Use-values → Metabolic functional form	Waste (processing and end of valued life) → Waste form
• non-metallic minerals • metals • fossil fuels • biomass	• food • feed • energy carriers • dissipative materials • stock building materials	• solid waste • biomass waste (corpses, excrements, feral life forms) • gaseous emissions • liquids and leachate
Sources/raw material//	Biophysical work/ use-value//	Sink/processed output//
extraction nexus	*productive and consumptive transformation nexus*	*waste nexus*

Source: Based on Fridolin Krausmann, Christian Lauk, Willi Haas and Dominik Wiedenhofer, "From Resource Extraction to Outflows of Wastes and Emissions: The Socio-economic Metabolism of the Global Economy, 1900–2015," *Global Environmental Change* 52 (September 2018): 131–140, https://doi.org/10.1016/j.gloenvcha.2018.07.003.

Based on the categories of material flow accounts, Table 1.1 organizes this differentiated mass flow according to the successive metamorphosis of the throughput as it passes through society, from raw materials, to functionally defined use-values, to its various waste forms. The last line of the table identifies the nexus of social relations that governs both the form and flow of the throughput as it goes through these metamorphoses.

With this in mind, we can now redraw the figure of the linear throughput taking into account the social relations that determine the mass flows of successive metamorphoses in Figure 1.8.

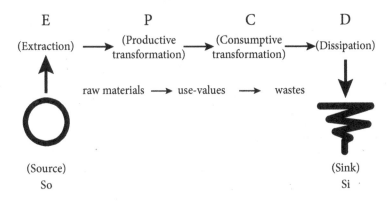

Figure 1.8   Metabolic model of the economic process as throughput
Source: Author.

This new representation of the throughput highlights a core feature of the metabolic model of the economic process on which is based the social ecology of capital. Whereas the classical understanding of the economic process is built around a two-point structure comprising "production" and "consumption," (P and C) held together by a circular flow of monetized value, the perspective of the social ecology of capital is a four-point process of extraction, production, consumption and dissipation held together by an irreversible linear throughput flow. All four moments are equally important to the economic process and none have a privileged position in the linear flow, each mediates and determines in a specific fashion the other points of the throughput as well as the structure as a whole, each is a nexus of socio-ecological relations that also mediates the relation of the economic process to sources (So) and sinks (Si), in each are entwined material and symbolic causalities, each is the site of a metamorphosis of the material flow. As shown in Figure 1.9, this four-point linear structure forms the foundation on which the analysis of the materiality of capitalist metabolism will rest in this work.

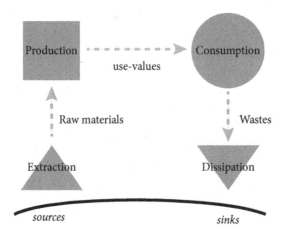

Figure 1.9   The four points of the economic process as throughput

Source: Author.

STOCKS: THE ACCUMULATION OF MATTER BY AND IN SOCIETY

Matter does not just flow through society, it accumulates in various forms as biophysical structures, or stocks. From a material accounting perspective, stocks can be defined as "ordered and interrelated biophysical entities created and reproduced by the continuous flows of energy and materials."[18] Conventional material flow accounts consider three types of biophysical stocks, meaning that matter accumulates inside society in three types of structures: human beings, livestock and material artifacts. The first two categories refer to the materiality of living bodies, both human and non-human, intentionally sustained by directed material and energy flows, their biological metabolism is socially mediated. The latter category encompasses those structures and material objects: buildings,

18.   Helmut Haberl, Dominik Wiedenhofer, Karl-Heinz Erb, Christoph Görg and Fridolin Krausmann, "The Material Stock–Flow–Service Nexus: A New Approach for Tackling the Decoupling Conundrum," *Sustainability* (Switzerland) 9(7) (2017): 4, https://doi.org/10.3390/su9071049.

infrastructures, machines, durable household goods, as well as works of art, that have been purposefully produced and reproduced through social activity. Artifacts differ from bodies in that they do not have a self-directed organic metabolism, nor self-purpose,[19] their objectivity—as artifacts—is social and cultural.

In contemporary societies, 55 percent of extracted matter is directed toward the accumulation of biophysical stocks, this includes almost all flows of non-metallic minerals (sand, gravel and limestone), most metal flows, and some biomass (paper, wood) and fossil-fuel flows (plastics).[20] A further characteristic of the materiality of contemporary societies is the importance of artifacts which outweigh by many orders of magnitude the mass of living bodies sustained by social activity and throughput flows. This contrasts with past societies where flows predominated over stocks and where bodies, animal and human, by far outweighed artifacts. Material growth in modern capitalist societies predominately takes the form of the accumulation of manufactured and constructed artifacts.

Objects exist as artifacts through the social relations projected onto their materiality as well as through the social activities that they mediate. This mediation can be productive; most artifacts in contemporary societies are products of social labor in its various forms. Artifacts as tools, machines and built structures in turn are essential mediations of productive activities in contemporary societies. But they also intervene as conditions of possibility or extensions of caring activities, of leisure, consumption and subsistence. Artifacts are "used," and this use, as discussed earlier concerning the elements of material flows, is socially determined and constructed through culture, meaning and institutions. This has led research to focus on the "services" to social life and economic activities provided by artifacts as a causal mechanism that explains their formation, accumulation and social reproduction, exploring the governance of their existence by an imperative of material functionality.[21] Highlighting the limits and perils of a merely functional understanding of social deter-

19. Alf Hornborg, "Artifacts Have Consequences, Not Agency: Toward a Critical Theory of Global Environmental History," *European Journal of Social Theory* 20(1) (2017): 95–110, https://doi.org/10.1177/1368431016640536.

20. Haberl et al., "The Material Stock–Flow–Service Nexus."

21. Christina Plank et al., "Doing More with Less: Provisioning Systems and the Transformation of the Stock–Flow–Service Nexus," *Ecological Economics* 187 (2021), https://doi.org/10.1016/j.ecolecon.2021.107093.

minations of material stock accumulation has led to the exploration of stocks as mediations of "routine practices" and their combination in daily life and structures of meaning.[22] A highway, a high-rise building, a computer terminal, a bulldozer, an SUV or a smart phone, to take a few pervasive artifacts that structure contemporary lives, embody in their material forms certain social practices and structures of meaning, all the while excluding or marginalizing others. Material stocks not only lock in and command certain practices by their form and presence, but they also empower certain classes of subjects and disempower others.[23]

From the perspective of the social ecology of capital, we will consider how imperatives of valorization determine the formation and reproduction of most stocks alongside the political, cultural and functional imperatives delineated above. In capitalist societies artifacts (as well as livestock) are the material form taken by the valued output as commodities and as fixed capital assets. Commodities must be sold and used up for their value to be realized, and fixed capital assets, including infrastructures and buildings, generate returns on investment over many productive cycles, as well as mediate the exploitation of labor. These capitalist imperatives shape how material stocks are produced, used, reproduced and destroyed. They do not correspond to the potential functional imperatives of material stock production, use and reproduction. In many instances, capital can impose a presumably dysfunctional determination to material stocks, planned obsolescence of household durables is a typical case. Property relations, labor relations and consumption norms institutionalize a specifically capitalist set of relations to material stock accumulation and determine in part the impact of stocks over the throughput flows. Accumulation of stocks is the materialization of accumulation of capital in contemporary societies.

Material stocks have some crucial *throughput effects*, the most important being the command they exercise over flows. An obvious command of stocks over flows is stock formation *per se*. Whether stocks are constructed or manufactured, their production is a flow of matter given form through labor. Once in existence, the specific form and volume of material

---

22. Helmut Haberl et al., "Stocks, Flows, Services and Practices: Nexus Approaches to Sustainable Social Metabolism," *Ecological Economics* 182 (2021): 106949–106949, https://doi.org/10.1016/j.ecolecon.2021.106949.
23. Haberl et al., "Stocks, Flows, Services and Practices."

stocks further commands and locks in flows that further determine both the mass (scale) and the composition of the throughput. In the case of livestock, this implies mass flows of feed from land that could have grown human food, but also mass outflows of methane form enteric digestion as well as manure and cadavers that must be sunk. To this must be added the flows of minerals and fossil fuels needed to produce the feed. These flows pale in comparison to the energy and material flows commanded by the artifacts of capitalist societies. The accumulation of machines, buildings and infrastructures that mediate productive and consumptive practices in contemporary societies depend on mass flows of fossil fuels to generate the energy needed to move, animate, cool, heat and power the systems embedded in these material stocks. Finally, stocks command flows not only through the production, use and activation of artifacts, but also because they themselves, as biophysical entities, "flow," continuously shedding matter which must be compensated by new material inputs until their end of life, or final dissipation. To sum up, stocks command flows through their production, use and reproduction, and the social relations that govern the existence of stocks (their production, use and reproduction) are the true loci of this material lock-in.

The dependence of stocks on specific flows leads to a second throughput effect. Throughput flows can limit and determine stock formation, use and their reproduction. Societies react to these limits by governing extractive and dissipative relations to ensure the existence and enable the production and accumulation of defined classes of material stocks. In capitalist societies, this has taken the form of the accumulation at the point of extraction and at the point of dissipation of artifacts specifically designed to govern the flow of matter as well as the forcing of sources and sinks. Examples abound in the mining sector as extractive technologies, infrastructures and machines are developed to exploit ever poorer sources of ores or deposits that for various reasons are more difficult to access. An extreme example is the development during the last decades of so-called "unconventional" methods of hydrocarbon extraction such as deep-sea wells, fracking and tar sands mining. Without these technological developments, the use and reproduction of a whole class of artifacts would prove next to impossible and this would have led to an important crisis of devalorization of fixed capital assets that depend on the continuous flow of oil and gas.

Accumulation can also take on an extreme form at the other end of the throughput flow, for example, in the development of infrastructures and machines specifically designed to capture and valorize greenhouse gases such as "carbon capture, use and sequestration" (CCUS) systems which both enhance the efficiency of oil and gas extraction through CO_2 injection in wells, and presumably prolong the use of hydrocarbon-based energy systems by managing their CO_2 sink problem. These examples illustrate a wider principle: capitalist societies do not passively react to the objective forces of resource scarcity; their reactions are much more complex. They actively govern their extractive and dissipative frontiers, and they do so by an accumulation of artifacts that take the form of fixed capital and these further lock in specific flow patterns, both in terms of material content, volume and flow-through rate.

A third throughput effect of stocks—artifacts in particular—rests on their relations to social practices.

Material stocks are accumulated as structures because they mediate diverse forms of social activities. Social relations of use are embedded in their material form, as are certain flow requirements. The command of stocks over flows is actualized through use: be it active such as driving a car, flushing a toilet or using a smart phone, or passive such as walking on a lit street or resting in a heated building. Social ecology has conceptualized this interrelation as a stock—flow—practice nexus, in which the command of stocks over flows brings them together with human—subjective—practice, labor in particular, but also consumption as well as expressive activities. This nexus is a three-tier structure as shown in Figure 1.10.

Figure 1.10 highlights the dialectical nature of the relation between practices and material stocks and flows, where each pole of the tier mediates the relations between the others, in the sense of exercising a form of causality. *Flows* limit and enable the use of stocks; *stocks* mediate the use of flows and *use* mediates the command of stocks over flows. The material relations of society always bring together these three tiers, and none exists independently of the others.

For social ecology, all forms of social activity are mediated by this material stock flow nexus, all the more so in a lifeworld suffused and structured by artifacts such as the world of advanced capitalism. But inversely, the stock flow nexus depicted above exists through the mediation of

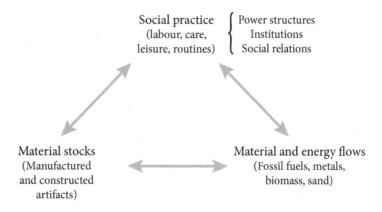

Figure 1.10   Metabolism as a stock flow practice nexus

Source: Helmut Haberl et al., "Stocks, Flows, Services and Practices: Nexus Approaches to Sustainable Social Metabolism," *Ecological Economics* 182 (2021): 106949.

social practice. The existence and use of artifacts is mediated by structures of meaning, or the symbolic, and social relations of domination and power.[24] This is true in all spheres of practice, even the most menial or seemingly thoughtless such as taking an elevator, drinking from a single use plastic straw, or choosing a powered leaf blower over a rake to manage fallen leaves. Among the complex of social relations that govern the nexus, we will focus on the institutions and practice that can be tied to the social structures of capitalist accumulation. In particular, we will highlight in Chapter 5 how social property relations regulate the stock–flow–practice nexus in advanced capitalist societies.

A SOCIAL ECOLOGY OF THE MATERIAL FLOW, A SUMMARY OF THE ARGUMENT SO FAR

The economic process of modern societies materializes as a linear throughput flow. This flow has some basic biophysical properties, as an abstract aggregate of matter, it has a scale and flows at a certain rate. The scale of the throughput is much larger than the valued output of a given economy, in the specific case of goods circulating in international trade, the throughput to output ratio can be a large as 25 to 1, but

---

24.   A methodological principle that goes back to Karl Marx's *The German Ideology.* New York: Prometheus Books, 1998.

on average hovers for the materials imported into the advanced capitalist core countries around 4 to 1. Both this ratio, and the overall mass of
the throughput at a global level has been growing over the last decades
and there is no indication that this will stop. Per capita measures of the
material footprint of the economic process of capitalist societies show
absolute throughput growth that cannot be attributed to a growing population of humans. This growth is especially strong in emerging centers
of the global capitalist economy such as China with the per capita
throughputs size multiplied by 4 in the last 25 years, but even the mature
economies of the advanced capitalist core in North America and Europe
have seen material footprint growth, per capita it has grown by 1.14 in
the former and 1.4 in the latter; only on the African continent has per
capita throughput growth stagnated. The throughput is growing relative
to the valued output, the throughput is growing relative to population
and the throughput is growing in absolute terms, from 27Gt of matter
extracted in 1970 to 92Gt in 2017, a growth of 3.39 over the period.
At this speed, the matter extracted and put into circulation by human
societies will outweigh the product of terrestrial net primary production
in the current decade.

The substance of the throughput is more complex than what can be
reduced to tonnes and joules; it has a prior composition at the point of
extraction and extracted matter is subject to a series of metamorphoses as it flows. It sheds and dons successive social forms and most imply
biophysical transformations. We will refer to these transformations as
the biophysical work of the material flow. The quantitative representation of the throughput is essential and crucial to capture and analyze the
biophysical scale of the economic process; it provides a synthetic representation of the materiality of capitalist economies as a mass flow. Part
of this flow accumulates inside society as material stocks. From a purely
analytical and biophysical standpoint, "a stock is a variable measured at a
specific point in time, whereas a flow is a variable measured over a period,
i.e. a unit of time."[25] Yet, from the perspective of social ecology, "stocks
are defined both physically [...] and socially, institutionally in the sense
that they belong to the social system and are continuously reproduced by

---

25. Haberl et al., "The Material Stock–Flow–Service Nexus," 1053.

activities of the social system."[26] So if the substance of the throughput is a flow of energy and matter, this flow coalesces into forms as artifacts that are determined by social relations of use. Use, be it productive or consumptive/reproductive, brings together into a nexus, artifacts (as material stocks), material and energy flows and human activity or practices in a meaningful and expressive manner. Use defines stocks as social and material forms, all the while artifacts enable and mediate defined forms of social practice, and both depend on and govern the linear flow. And this dialectic always implies further flows of energy and matter in a *stock flow practice nexus*. This three-tiered structure is the form taken on by the metabolic relations of the economic process in capitalist societies (and one could argue in all societies where an economic process is discernible through institutional differentiation of this sphere).

We have seen earlier in our basic model of the economic process that the material flow is marked by four successive structural moments: extraction, production, consumption and dissipation, each of which, we argued, is the site of specific socio-economic relations that mediate the overall throughput. We can now refine our basic model by noting that these relations take on a "stock flow practice nexus" form, each of these structural moments or points of the economic process can be defined as a configuration between artifacts, flows and social practices; each is a nexus and it is as such that each determines and mediates the throughput from source to sink. We have seen how the material flow changes form as it passes from one structural moment to another; the same metamorphoses determine the other elements of the nexus: social practices and accumulated stocks in particular. Stocks in the extractive, productive and dissipative structures of the throughput flow exist primarily as fixed capital subject to a valorization imperative; practices in these spheres take on the social form of labor and employment. In the sphere of consumption, stocks appear as durable goods and residential structures as well as collectively consumed public infrastructures, practices are mixed, consumption, provisioning, care, leisure and creative—expressive activities. Finally, in a capitalist society, extraction, production, consumption and dissipation are not only sites of material stock accumulation, of the nexus

---

26. Marina Fischer-Kowalski and Helmut Haberl, "Social Metabolism: A Metric for Biophysical Growth and Degrowth," in Joan Martínez-Alier and Roldan Muradian (eds.), *Handbook of Ecological Economics.* Cheltenham: Edward Elgar, 2015, 102.

of artifacts, flows and social practices, these structural moments of the linear throughput are also tied together in the process of capital accumulation and growth in a capitalist society is a result of the dialectic between these two dimensions of economic and social reality.

2

Nature's Work:
The Ecology of the Material Flow

Work, alongside labor, is a complex category and reality in modern societies; its common everyday usage relates to purposeful social activities requiring effort, attention, some skill and is directed toward an end that has an objective nature.[1] In physics, work is defined through a simple formula as energy transferred to or from an object by force rather than through the random movements of particles—which is the definition of heat.[2] Work results in a changed physical reality, again in its simplest form as displacement of an object to which force is applied in space. This definition constructed during the nineteenth century evolved out of the more vernacular use of the word as a category of practice in everyday life. In a sense work, as understood by physics, emerged by a process of abstraction, and in lieu of this was the observation by those who developed physical science of mechanical processes in manufacturing, mining, in particular, where steam power was first applied at an industrial scale. Work as the abstract "capacity to effect physical reality in a directed manner" by machines, bodies and objects evolved out of capitalist relations of production and became a foundational concept of modern thermodynamics.[3] Nature works, and we will explore in the following pages the biophysical work expected of the mass throughput commanded by contemporary societies.

It has become commonplace among critical ecological theories of capitalism to account for the contribution of nature to the economic process

---

1. See, for example, the entry "Work," in Raymond Williams, *Keywords: A Vocabulary of Culture and Society*. New York: Oxford University Press, 1976; and Hannah Arendt, *The Human Condition*. Chicago, IL: University of Chicago Press, 1958.
2. Donald T. Haynie, *Biological Thermodynamics*. Cambridge: Cambridge University Press, 2008. See also Vaclav Smil, *Energy and Nature and Society: General Energetics of Complex Systems*. Cambridge, MA: MIT Press, 2008.
3. Cara N. Daggett, *The Birth of Energy: Fossil Fuels, Thermodynamics, and the Politics of Work*. Durham, NC: Duke University Press, 2019.

by positing the exploitation or subsumption of natural processes by capitalist relations of production and appropriation. This has led to revisionist theories of value: for some, this implies considering nature's contribution to the formation of exchange value alongside labor,[4] while for others, such as Jason Moore it means more globally that "capitalist ecologies" are essential to the accumulation process.[5] We share with these theoretical efforts the view that the materialistic critique of capitalist societies must be ecologized, yet we do not espouse the view that something such as natural labor can exist, that this concept, or any attempt to naturalistically ground exchange value, either in energy or ecology, is analytically productive.[6] Two epistemological propositions follow from these principles.

First, nature works, but does not labor, nature is not underpaid, nor is nature's labor "cheap" and it is not a source of exchange value. These are all categories that belong to the sphere of a monetary production economy, where money mediates social relations of production and circulation between subjects that belong to a community of payment.[7] In capitalism, labor is what work becomes when it is valued, and this primarily happens through monetary exchange and the subsumption of productive activity by a capitalist labor process. Other forms of work are, from a capitalist viewpoint, without value even though they might be socially necessary.[8]

---

4. See, for example, the interesting debate between Giorgos Kallis and Erik Swyngedouw, Giorgos "Do Bees Produce Value? A Conversation Between an Ecological Economist and a Marxist Geographer," *Capitalism Nature Socialism* 29(3) (2018): 36–50, https://doi.org/10.1080/10455752.2017.1315830.

5. Jason W. Moore, *Capitalism in the Web of Life: Ecology and the Accumulation of Capital*. New York: Verso, 2015.

6. The hybridist attempt to do away with the nature–society dialectic through the attribution of actancy to natural processes when combined with social processes ends up making the same argument but in a more convoluted manner. For a critique of these attempts to develop a naturalistic theory of value—all the while denying the existence of naturalism as an epistemological position—see John Bellamy Foster and Paul Burkett, "Value Isn't Everything," *Monthly Review* 70(6) (2018), https://monthlyreview.org/2018/11/01/value-isnt-everything/.

7. Even when paying for ecosystem services, the ultimate recipient of the monetary payment will not be "nature," nor the ecosystem, nor even a particular being such as a plant or an animal; it will be a legal person, embodied either in a human being or in an organization such as a non-profit corporation.

8. We share with Biesecker and Hofmeister the theory that value is not a substance found in objects, or inherent to productive activities in general. Value is an institution that mediates the objectivity of work as labor as much as it transforms the mode of existence of objects and does so through the boundary or frontier it constructs between the valorized and the devalorized. The universality of the capitalist value-form of labor

In other modes of production and social formations, work becomes labor according to different normative rules and social relations of valuation.

Second, capitalism *has* ecological relations, but it is not an ecology, and nature's work is an essential dimension of these relations. A full analysis of how nature works for capitalist societies and how capitalism puts nature to work would be an encyclopedic project in and of itself. Here we explore the much more limited problem of the biophysical work expected of the linear throughput through a discussion of thermodynamics and the physics of ecology. The results of this inquiry lay the basis for a socio-ecological theory of the metabolism of societies that is presented in the concluding part of the chapter and which is further developed in Chapters 3 and 4.

THERMODYNAMICS AS BIOPHYSICAL WORK

As the throughput flows from one point of the economic process to another, it accomplishes biophysical work which is subject to the laws of thermodynamics. Taking into account these laws and the work performed by the throughput—either as a stock or a flow—has been a defining feature of the biophysical branch of ecological economics since the pioneering studies of Nicholas Georgescu-Roegen and Robert Ayres in the 1970s.[9] Use can be considered an actualization of a biophysical potential of a material element, the everyday understanding of use contains the idea of something being "used" or "used up," a biophysical potential that—from the standpoint of human practice and experience—has been entirely actualized and is extinguished. The modern category of "consumption" implies the same set of ideas. But in the real everyday world of capitalist economies and societies, the frontier between use and waste, or consumption and dissipation is overdetermined by social processes and relations that may have nothing to do with this biophysical "use" and

is a contested social relation in modern society where other valorization regimes of social activity exist and are politically or culturally mediated, care labor is a typical case. Adelheid Biesecker and Sabine Hofmeister, "Focus: (Re)productivity Sustainable Relations Both Between Society and Nature and Between the Genders," *Ecological Economics* 69(8) (2010): 1703–1711.

9. Nicholas Georgescu-Roegen, *The Entropy Law and the Economic Process.* Cambridge, MA: Harvard University Press, 1971; and Robert U. Ayres and Allen V. Kneese, "Production, Consumption, and Externalities," *American Economic Review* 59(3) (1969): 282–297.

everything to do with capitalist imperatives of valorization and, most of all, of realization of value. We will examine the subsumption of use by capitalist imperatives in detail in Chapters 5 and 6. At this point of our argument, we will study that which is subsumed, the biophysical work of the throughput elements.

The throughput flow of capitalist societies is a thermodynamic process. What does this imply? That the economic process is subjected to the two laws of thermodynamics: the first being the law of conservation; and the second being the entropy law. These laws apply to both matter and energy, the substance of the throughput. As the throughput flows from source to sink, from extraction to dissipation, its quantity does not change, or as Antoine de Lavoisier would state in what is considered the founding treatise of modern chemistry in 1789: *nothing is lost, nothing is created, all is transformed.*[10] The economic implications of the first law have been highlighted by Robert Ayres: "You can't get something from nothing, and you can't convert something into nothing."[11] This means, that though monetary value can be created, accumulated and destroyed during the economic process, the material and energy throughput can only be transformed. The nature of this transformation, what we named the metamorphosis of the throughput in Chapter 1, will be examined here when studying the economic implications of the second law. The structural moments of the economic process that we have outlined in Chapter 1—extraction, production, consumption and dissipation—correspond to four successive biophysical "transformations" of the throughput.

A second observation is that outside of nuclear reactions such as fission or fusion, matter and energy exist as independent entities. They are measured, put to work and transformed separately. Matter cannot become energy, nor can energy become matter. In the economic process, energy and matter work together, both are needed and in capitalist production and consumption, they are bound as fixed coefficients locked into the nexus of fixed capital and produced artifacts. This fix is both quantitative and qualitative. The use of artifacts depends on combinations of given forms or kinds of matter and energy, not only of given amounts. In

---

10. Antoine de Lavoisier, *Traité élémentaire de chimie, présenté dans un ordre nouveau et d'après les découvertes modernes.* Paris: Cuchet, 1789.
11. Robert U. Ayres and Benjamin Warr, *The Economic Growth Engine: How Energy and Work Drive Material Prosperity.* Cheltenham: Edward Elgar, 2009, 64.

capitalist economies, this technical rigidity is further amplified as these combinations are capitalized by monopolistic corporations as productive or consumptive artifacts. A last implication comes from the mass balance principle that follows from the first law, succinctly: what has been extracted will be dissipated. Waste flows are locked into the throughput by extractive flows. This can be differed in time through stock accumulation; the material form of the extractive flows might be transformed, but in the end massive extraction is reflected in massive waste and dissipation. The climate crisis is, of course, an obvious and dramatic example of this principle.

The second law of thermodynamics has more far-reaching implications for the study of the economic process and has been more widely debated both in ecological economics,[12] and in critical political economy.[13] The subject of much controversy, for the purposes of our analysis, we will focus on the phenomenological definition of entropy presented by Georgescu-Roegen: "in an isolated system, the amount of energy remains constant (the first law), while the available energy continuously and irrevocably degrades into unavailable states."[14] Availability is a phenomenological concept; it refers to the degradation of the quality of energy as it performs useful work from the standpoint of human society.[15]

For Georgescu-Roegen, this process of entropic degradation also applies to matter. As it is transformed by the economic process, matter irrevocably loses qualities which he equates to *"orderliness"*: all the while conserving its mass, matter changes from a state of order to a state of disorder or maximum dispersal and this change is irreversible.[16] The

---

12. Rigo E. Melgar-Melgar and Charles A.S. Hall, "Why Ecological Economics Needs to Return to its Roots: The Biophysical Foundation of Socio-Economic Systems," *Ecological Economics* 169 (2020), https://doi.org/10.1016/j.ecolecon.2019.106567.

13. See Paul Burkett and John Bellamy Foster, "Metabolism, Energy, and Entropy in Marx's Critique of Political Economy: Beyond the Podolinsky Myth," *Theory and Society* (35) (2006): 109–156, https://doi.org/10.1007/s11186-006-6781-2.

14. Nicholas Georgescu-Roegen, "The Entropy Law and the Economic Process in Retrospect," *Eastern Economic Journal* 12(1) (1986): 3, www.jstor.org/stable/40357380.

15. This phenomenological definition of the second law could be extended to the experiential field of all living beings, given that life rests on the capacity of reproduction of orderly organic structures by increasing the entropy in its physical environment. We will discuss this more fully further on.

16. Georgescu-Roegen, "The Entropy Law and the Economic Process in Retrospect," 3. The concept of orderliness as an absolute physical state of matter that exists and can be formally represented irrespective of human activity, and then the theory of

central argument of his ecological economics could be formulated thus: as matter and energy flow through the successive transformations of the economic process they change from a state of *orderliness or low entropy to disorderliness and dispersal or high entropy, and this change is irreversible.* To seize the full implication of the second law of thermodynamics for a social ecology of capital and a theory of biophysical work it is important to examine initially two aspects of the above definition: the notion of the economic process as a "closed system" and the "phenomenological" nature of the second law. We will start with the latter problem.

THERMODYNAMICS AS A PHENOMENOLOGY OF NATURE'S WORK

Since Georgescu-Roegen's last studies of the economic significance of the entropy law in the late 1980s, there have been a number of important works that have studied the socio-cultural, economic and political context in which thermodynamics in particular and the physics of energy in general emerged and developed.[17] While reviewing this body of scholarship is outside of the scope of the present work, there is one important aspect that we must acknowledge and which is central to a sociologically informed phenomenological approach to thermodynamics. As argued both by Larry Lohmann and Cara Daggett, the science of energy and thermodynamics cannot be understood outside their social context of emergence, which in this case is the historical emergence and expansion of industrial capitalism and capitalist colonialism.[18] The exploitation of land and labor as factors of production in the valorization process of capital did more than "color" the categories of modern physics, it shaped its core concepts. And thus, the problem of the entropic degradation of energy is intimately tied to the historical experience of organizing tech-

---

entropy as an irreversible change toward disorder, has been questioned as an appropriate understanding of the second of thermodynamics. A phenomenological use of the concept on the other hand as "order for us," is appropriate and it is in this sense that the concept is used here.

17.   Daggett, *The Birth of Energy*; and Larry Lohmann and Nicholas Hildyard, *Energy, Work and Finance*. Sturminster Newton: The Corner House, 2014, available at: www. thecornerhouse.org.uk/sites/thecornerhouse.org.uk/files/EnergyWorkFinance%20 %282.57MB%29.pdf.

18.   Daggett, *The Birth of Energy*; and Lohmann and Hildyard, *Energy, Work and Finance*.

nologies of mass energy conversions from "prime movers" to "useful work." The capacity to convert forms of energy from one to another— heat to mechanical (coal into steam), mechanical to kinetic (steam to turbine), kinetic to electric (turbine to electricity), electric to heat (baseboard heating systems in US and Canadian homes) or mechanical work (such as folding metal sheets into baseboard heating frames)—led to the emergence of the abstract category of energy as a unified "thing" present in living bodies and in inert matter that could be "harnessed" and "put to work."[19] Technologies of conversion and measure (including the ones used in this book) contributed to the historical construction of representations of energy in the eighteenth and nineteenth centuries as this abstract and amorphous "capacity to do work."

The first law of thermodynamics meant that energy as an abstract substance survived the work of its particular and ephemeral manifestations such as heat, movement, pressure or chemical reactions. As a quantity, it was conserved. Yet, as stated by the second law, each change of form was a degradation of its quality understood as its capacity to do useful work. At one point the initial quantum of energy would simply be unavailable to society, all the while still existing in a physical sense. And thus usefulness, or availability, though a physical principle and natural law, exists from the standpoint of the human desire or social need for energy to perform work, meaning to induce some form of biophysical change. This is what Georgescu-Roegen meant by the phenomenological nature of the entropy law—we could add with Larry Lohmann and Cara Daggett—only in modern capitalist (and state socialist) society has this category of energy as an abstract substance that is both conserved and degraded, emerged and imposed itself as representation of work.

OPEN AND CLOSED SYSTEMS

Thermodynamic laws apply to closed systems, and thus the principles delineated above are relevant because the observed processes—the economy as a material process—appear as bounded. Whether this boundedness is considered as a biophysical reality or the product of an act, observation is irrelevant from the standpoint of thermodynamics, again because of the phenomenological nature of thermodynamic science. As

---

19. Lohmann and Hildyard, *Energy, Work and Finance.*

Georgescu-Roegen notes in his 1985 lecture "strictly speaking, the only isolated system is the whole universe" and in this system the thermodynamic laws take on the form given to them by Rudolf Clausius:

the energy of the universe is constant [Law 1] and
the entropy of the universe tends to a maximum [Law 2][20]

Interesting and relevant though this may be from the perspective of theoretical physics, it is the thermodynamic consequences of the boundedness of the Earth that are of import for societies and their ecology. Energetically the Earth is an open system, open to the flux of solar radiation. As this energy enters the planet's atmosphere, it is degraded and leaves as dissipated heat. Though the sun itself is subject to the entropy law and will eventually die out, it can be assumed to be eternal when examined from the timescale of human societies and even more so from the much shorter temporal horizon of our current ecological crisis. The sun's energetic output, its potential, is at the heart of current debates concerning the ecological transition confronting economies and societies. It is, after all, the essential source of available energy on this planet. Apart from geothermal, chemical, tidal and nuclear energy, all other sources of useful energetic work depend on current or past solar influx. This flux can be considered constant for the Earth as a whole (though there are diurnal and seasonal variations according to latitude and longitude).[21] It is responsible for the main kinetic geophysical processes that mark the Earth system such as wind, water currents and precipitation, which outside of tectonics, animate and shape the planet. So long as the sun shines, the winds blow and rivers flow, the irreversibility of the entropic degradation of solar energy into an outgoing flux of heat does not seem

20. Rudolf Clausius, *Ninth Memoir: On Several Convenient Forms of the Fundamental Equations of the Mechanical Theory of Heat* (1867).
21. There are variations which correspond to slight oscillations in the Earth's orbital trajectory, and these are responsible for the glacial and interglacial Milankovitch cycles—although these variations fall outside of the scope of our analysis. The human societies we are examining have flourished in the latest interglacial and the Earth's climate has been forced to a degree that sets it onto a warming trajectory outside of these cycles. Will Steffen et al., "Trajectories of the Earth System in the Anthropocene," Proceedings of the National Academy of Sciences of the United States of America, 115(33) (2018): 8252–8259, www.pnas.org/doi/pdf/10.1073/pnas.1810141115.

to be a dramatic problem for a society that can base its energetic demands on these geophysical processes. This is something capitalist societies have not been able to do up until now and nor does it seem probable in the near future.[22] The energetic basis of capitalist growth and accumulation since 1800 has been a limited stock of fossil fuels extracted from the Earth, not the generous influx of solar energy or at least not directly. Buried sunshine has been a common metaphor used in environmental discourse to describe geological deposits of coal, oil and gas that result from past capture and conversion of the solar influx of energy through photosynthesis. In this sense, capitalist growth is based on an influx of energy from the sun and thus on the Earth as an open system, but an openness mediated by life.

This mediation has literally changed the face of the planet. The conversion of the solar influx through photosynthesis is the basis of almost all possible biotic activity through metabolic processes which represent biochemical work.[23] Life has been called a "negentropic" force which changes the patterns of the entropic degradation of the solar energy flux here on Earth, without canceling or suspending the laws of thermodynamics. This negentropic force sustains and produces organic structures—biomass—and planetary biogeochemical cycles which have become key components of the Earth as a "living" open system. "Life feeds on low entropy 'food' and rejects high entropy 'waste' products and heat, thereby fueling its metabolism and sustaining its structure."[24] This can be considered a basic metabolic law of all living entities; it applies to the Earth system as a whole, redefining its boundedness as an ecological rather than only a geophysical reality. As an ecologically mediated open system, the living earth rests on the capture of the constant influx of solar energy by photosynthesis and the dense ecological relations that have developed around the use and circulation of the produced energy

22. Megan K. Seibert and William E. Rees, "Through the Eye of a Needle: An Eco-Heterodox Perspective on the Renewable Energy Transition," *Energies* 14(15) (2021): 4508, https://doi.org/10.3390/en14154508.
23. On this, see the modelization of these processes. Kleidon, A. (2010). "Life, Hierarchy, and the Thermodynamic Machinery of Planet Earth." *Physics of Life Reviews* 7(4): 424–460. See also Joseph E. Armstrong. *How the Earth Turned Green: A Brief 3.8-Billion-Year History of Plants.* Chicago, IL: University of Chicago Press, 2014.
24. Axel Kleidon, "Life, Hierarchy, and the Thermodynamic Machinery of Planet Earth," *Physics of Life Reviews* 7(4) (October 2010): 427, https://doi.org/10.1016/j.plrev.2010.10.002.

and organized matter through trophic functions of primary production, consumption and decomposition. Combined with geophysical forces that also depend on the solar flux of energy such as weathering and hydrological cycles, trophic functions ensure the availability of critical chemical nutrients for life processes and come together as the basic biogeochemical cycles of the planet, the carbon cycle, phosphorous and nitrogen as well as sulfur cycles. These relations responsible for the circulation of nutrients critical to life in organic structures form a totality that regulates the Earth's climate, the composition of the atmosphere, of oceans as well of the soils that form the ground on which we stand.[25]

The reproduction of the planet's ecosystems and of all living beings is embedded in these living Earth processes, it is also in these organic structures that our societies are embedded. The ecology of our societies is in great part based on these relations. And because the Earth as a living system is open to the sun's energetic flux, and life metabolically transforms this energy into structures and processes that are able to conserve and recycle critical nutrients through trophic systems, this introduces a semblance of reversibility in a physical world otherwise condemned to entropic degradation. A fitting representation is that of an organic circular structure typical of most ecosystems where decomposition of wastes is a precondition for a new cycle of primary production. This contrasts strongly with the representation of the economic process of societies as a linear flow that we have presented in Chapter 1. Yet, this apparent organic circularity, it must be remembered, rests on a constant influx of energy from the sun and on its capture through photosynthesis.

Ecosystems, living beings and the living earth system as a whole, are all, at their various scales of existence, dissipative structures able to "maintain their state away from thermodynamic equilibrium [equivalent to death for a living body] by an overall net export of entropy to the surroundings." This is true of all metabolic processes, including social metabolism, however seemingly circular.[26]

---

25. On the significance of this way of understanding the Earth as a dynamic system, see Ian Angus, *Facing the Anthropocene: Fossil Capitalism and the Crisis of the Earth System*. New York: Monthly Review Press, 2016. For a more technical and synthetic presentation, see Johan Rockström et al., "Planetary Boundaries: Exploring the Safe Operating Space for Humanity," *Ecology and Society* 14(2) (2009), www.ecologyandsociety.org/vol14/iss2/art32/.

26. Life and ecological relations do not produce "negative entropy" as some political ecologists have affirmed. Stability is gained locally at the expense of greater entropy

Furthermore, the linear flow of contemporary societies is only partially tied to net primary production and its organic negentropy and trophic circularity. As seen in Chapter 1, three-quarters (74 percent for 2017) of the global throughput flow is abiotic in nature and exists as an ensemble of extractable material stocks: non-metallic minerals such as potash, phosphates, sand, gravel and limestone used to make concrete, fossil fuels and various metals. Though the availability of many of these substances as low entropy and ordered matter is in part the result of *past* biotic activity— for fossil fuels this is obvious, but also for some forms of minerals such as dolomitic limestone and metals such as limonite—from the material standpoint of the extractive needs and practices of capitalist economies, they appear as finite geological stocks and our planet appears as a closed, bounded and largely inert—non-organic—geological system.[27]

True the Earth as a geophysical system does have its cycles and dynamic processes, plate tectonics, as well as weathering, erosion and sedimentation which are induced by the solar energy flux, but these geological processes are slow, extending over eons and eras, not days, seasons and years when compared to the fast temporality of ecological cycles with their daily and seasonal rhythms. We can existentially and experientially relate to even the slowest of organic growth cycles—such as trees—which have some degree of commensurability with human timescales and can be counted in generations, whereas our cultures have not developed an experiential framework that captures the orogenic growth of mountain ranges. As argued by Jeremy Davies, human societies experience ecological cycles temporally as processes, they experience geology as a fixed frame and geological change as catastrophic events.[28] Geological sources of useful matter appear from the perspective of the linear throughput

elsewhere, and societies cannot through technologies reverse the course of entropy. There is no escape or exception to the laws of thermodynamics, at least in this universe, and even the act of imagining a parallel one where these laws would not apply is an entropic process.

27. Martin Arboleda, *Planetary Mine: Territories of Extraction under Late Capitalism*. London: Verso, 2020.

28. Jeremy Davies, *The Birth of the Anthropocene*. Oakland, CA: University of California Press, 2016. This is, of course, changing as the experience of socially induced climate change moves from the sphere of scientific debates and discoveries to the culture of everyday life, though this shift remains dependent on scientific mediation: Alan E. Stewart and Jungsu Oh, "Weather and Climate as Events: Contributions to the Public Idea of Climate Change," *International Journal of Big Data Mining for Global Warming* 1(2) (2019): 1950005, https://doi.org/10.1142/S2630534819500050.

flow as finite and subject to the entropy law, or more precisely in accordance with the first and second laws of thermodynamics. It is because of entropy that geological sources of useful matter appear as stocks that can be used up rather than flows. This boundedness of the earth as a store of finite, low entropy, extractable matter is thus also a phenomenological reality rooted in the economic experience of societies. When put to work, either as feedstocks for industrial processes, as energy carriers or other dissipative uses such as in agriculture, or accumulated as construction materials fixed in infrastructures, buildings or in manufactured artifacts, matter undergoes an entropic degradation as a counterpart of its usefulness or capacity to work.

The second law of thermodynamics, like the first, provides a solid foundation for an account of nature's work in the economic process understood as a linear throughput flow. We have summed these up in the following five principles:

1. what appears as the useful work of energy and matter from the perspective of society is based on biophysical work of *low entropy* inputs into the economic process;

2. biophysical work in all its forms (including human and animal labor) implies entropic degradation and dissipation of energy and matter, the economic process transforms low entropy inputs from "sources" into *high entropy* wastes directed to "sinks";

3. entropic degradation and dissipation are irreversible processes and any material reversibility such as recycling, rests on ever greater expenditures of energy and additional inputs of matter, full circularity of matter and energy does not exist in a world governed by the laws of thermodynamics;

4. the processual nature of economic activity that governs the throughput flow is less a question of *temporal* irreversibility and more one of *entropic* irreversibility;

5. because the biosphere is an open system, ecological processes do have a form of organic circularity based on the principle of negentropy through trophic cycles and primary production. This is not true of economic processes based on the extraction and entropic transformation of geological stocks of matter, including energy carriers such as fossil fuels, that formed the material base of capitalist accumulation in the last two centuries.

ENTROPY HAPPENS

Entropy becomes socio-economically significant for a society that depends on a mode of production based on the extraction and metamorphoses of geological stocks of matter and the work of stocks of fossilized energy carriers. *In fine* the entropy law expresses the biophysical limits of capitalist societies[29] that have come to depend on this material base for their growth and accumulation. Figure 2.1, based on Figure 1.1 of the linear throughput in Chapter 1, presents the materiality of the economic process as an entropic process.

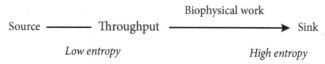

Figure 2.1   Throughput as biophysical work
Source: Author.

As the throughput flows, it moves from a state of low to high entropy and this is an irreversible process of degradation of the quality of matter and energy even though their quantity is conserved. The irreversibility of the flow is not primarily temporal, it is entropic. This also means that each of the formal moments of the economic process outlined previously: extraction, production, consumption and dissipation also correspond to an entropic process, or put another way they now appear as biophysical transformations that take shape as biophysical work and are also thus entropic in nature (Figure 2.2).

Yet, this entropic economic process is also embedded in ecosystems and planetary biogeochemical cycles which, from the perspective of society, have a circular negentropic form. Biophysical work by these organic systems appears along the metabolic frontier between the economic process and the natural systems of the living earth, generating biomass-based sources and through ecological processes absorbing sunk wastes. These ecological relations of societies impact these systems

---

29. As argued by Georgescu-Roegen, this constraint also applies to state socialist economies that adopted the same material base and made growth of the valued output their overall economic objective. Even though valuation in this case was based on use-value rather than exchange value.

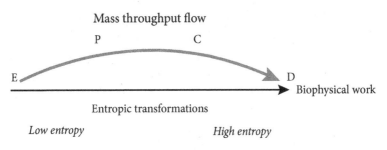

Figure 2.2   Mass throughput flow as entropy
Source: Author.

through their scale and the nature of their interactions. Extraction, whether it be harvest of biotic and organic matter or mined and collected as abiotic products of geological cycles, transforms trophic relations in ecosystems and more widely impacts them through land use change such as agriculture and cultivated forests, as well as provoking fragmentation of natural communities. Accumulation of stocks radically transforms space through urbanization, replacing complex ecosystems with artificialized, simplified or impoverished ecological communities. And dissipation implies mass inflows of high entropy waste into ecosystems and their integration into biogeochemical cycles. Ecosystems and biogeochemical cycles, more so the living Earth system as a whole, can co-evolve with the metabolism of the economic process maintaining stability and resilience, or it can be forced into instability and non-linear change, which is what we see today in the case of the carbon, nitrogen and phosphorous cycles. Non-linear change can also take the form of the collapse of ecosystems such as coral reefs, forests or wetlands. With Marx and contemporary eco-Marxists such as John Bellamy Foster, we can speak of an ecological *rift* when the coupling of economic processes and ecological relations destabilizes the integrity and viability of ecosystems and forces Earth processes into zones of dramatic non-linear change or tipping points.

A LAST NOTE ON METABOLISM AND SOCIAL ECOLOGY

Metabolism in general, whether social or biological, rests on the conversion of solar energy by plants through photosynthetic activity. This conversion is the basis for almost all living activity on Earth. The biosphere would be a very marginal structure if it were not for the primary production of organic matter by plants and its by-product, breathable oxygen. "Net primary production" (NPP) measures the amount of biomass that results from photosynthesis, the biophysical surplus of captured and converted solar energy, above and beyond what plants and other auto-trophs expend to maintain their metabolic functions. A particularity of NPP is that plants directly store as bodily mass the net solar energy they capture and convert—this happens through *organic growth*. And, as they grow, plants also assimilate into their tissues and bodies, minerals critical to life processes, in both large (N, P, K) and trace amounts, which they capture with the help of symbionts such as rhizobium bacteria and mycorrhiza, among others. Both this energy and these minerals are then available to other living beings through trophic relations that come together as ecosystems. We can divide life on Earth between the auto-trophs, which produce NPP, and all other beings, heterotrophs, be they herbivores that feed off autotrophic growth, carnivores who feed off the latter or detritivores responsible for the ultimate cycling of biomass and essential nutrients. Plants have been characterized as an "unparalleled energy store" and, if we include those marine autotroph fossils that today appear to us as fossil-fuel reserves, this is fundamentally true.[30] Plants and their aquatic relatives are the foundation of the biosphere's web of life and a fountain of available energy and matter that all other life forms must tap into. From the perspective of the metabolism of living beings, the NPP of autotrophs forms a totality, a measurable whole that limits in the absolute, through trophic networks, organic growth and the activity of all beings. The metabolism of human societies, up until the integration of fossil fuels and nuclear energy into the throughput, was also entirely bounded by NPP. And as living heterotrophs, we remain dependent on NPP for our food. As we saw in Chapter 1, we harvest and transform biomass for a much wider variety of uses and practices than simply food.

Yet, we cannot reduce the ecological contribution of plants only to pro-visioning the biosphere with a surplus of biomass and energy. Primary production is also an essential regulation of climatological processes and hydrological cycles. Plant life is a critical regulatory mechanism of

---

30. Rolf Peter Sieferle, *The Subterranean Forest: Energy Systems and the Industrial Revolution*. Cambridge: White Horse Press, 2001, 2.

the Earth's most basic biogeochemical cycles.[31] Living beings, whether autotrophs or heterotrophs, have been described in our discussion of thermodynamics as dissipative structures who maximize entropy production to maintain their unity and biophysical integrity as living organisms. Yet, from the standpoint of the biosphere, one can describe the activity of living beings as a whole as the transformation of the linear entropic flux of solar energy onto Earth into a circular flow of biomass, critical nutrients and energy. A circular flow growing organic structures and regulating planetary processes that all together make the earth a living planet. Life, through its ecological relations, mediates both the thermodynamic openness and closure of this Earth system, flourishing inside biophysical limits of its own making and keeping the planet well away from the thermodynamic equilibrium that should characterize its state given its position in the solar system and the composition of its abiotic elements. We could reduce this natural work to the provision of ecosystem services to humanity, and assign a monetary value to this work through various techniques, some more dubious than others. But, following Marx's intuition, it is much more interesting to consider this resulting circularity as an ecological foundation that has sustained the flourishing of life and development of its expressive capacities.

This was a perspective on ecology and natural history developed by Murray Bookchin's social ecology in the 1980s, in particular in his *Ecology of Freedom* and also in his essays on "dialectical naturalism." There he argued that the flourishing of life was driven by a quasi-teleological drive toward greater diversity, reflexivity and ultimately freedom, which in nature assumed the more basic form of spontaneity. He also projected onto nature an inherent tendency of development of cooperative and mutualistic relationships, an idea which today is at the center of our understanding of the ecology of soils and their associated herbaceous or forest communities. Here might be an appropriate place to distinguish the social ecology developed in these pages from this aspect of Bookchin's thought. We agree with his view that an evolutionary thrust toward greater richness and diversity of the interdependencies between

---

31.   Finally, an essential contribution of plant life to the terrestrial biosphere is their participation in the formation and reproduction of living soils, host to a complex web of beings that keep essential minerals to life and carbon flowing in trophic networks— soils that remain essential foundations of the metabolism of all societies.

living beings in ecosystems is apparent, and we also consider the resulting dense and complex trophic webs as a dialectical whole where matter and energy circulate, where organic structures accumulate and ecological relations contribute to the regulation of planet wide biophysical cycles and processes that literally make our world. Yet, here we break away from Bookchin: this totality need not be. And, in fact, the planet as an ecological whole has collapsed on occasion in its long history, evolution is contingent, mass extinctions of catastrophic scale happen. The same trend marks the historical process of human societies, its progressiveness is contingent and need not be, nor should human societies develop "first nature like" cooperative and non-hierarchical relations and structures. They *can* develop such a culture, and actually much of our daily lives is structured by a basal communism that resembles Bookchin's anarchic normativity. This ethos of care and commoning is a social question which cannot be founded on any naturalistic principle. Hierarchy, as an organizing principal of social relations, is no less natural than its absence. The expressive and normative autonomy of societies, much as that of life itself, is the only ontological foundation of their historicity.[32] This would be the main distance between the views developed by Bookchin and the argument developed here.

---

32. Michel Freitag, *Introduction à une théorie générale du symbolique: dialectique et société*, Vol. 2. Montreal: Liber, 2011.

3

Metabolic Regimes in a Historical Perspective

ECOLOGY AND GEOLOGY

We can—phenomenologically—divide Earth system processes according to two different timescales. In Chapter 2, we drew a distinction between those processes which are conditioned by diurnal and seasonal variations as well as annual patterns of organic growth, and others which unfold in geological time-frames, a distinction between ecological cycles and geological cycles. We can also distinguish these as "fast" and "slow" biogeochemical cycles and Earth processes, one governed by life and biological activity and others regulated by processes that evolve according to timescales and that are subsumed by abiotic processes we understand as geological.[1] All societies up until the present have found in the fast ecological cycles their limit as well as the basis for their flourishing and the expression of diverse modes of living. One way to understand the distinction between capitalist fossil metabolism and its agrarian antecedents is that capitalism during the last two centuries and a half has as a limiting factor to its development and growth the capacity to tap into geological (slow) cycles for critical elements of its metabolism,[2] whereas agrarian

---

1. As we argued in Chapter 2, life and living activity contributes to both: the fast ecological cycles are determined by the thermodynamic constraint to capture, transform, circulate and dissipate as well as accumulate as biomass solar energy; and the slow geological cycles though driven by abiotic forces such as the energy flux from the Earth's core, as well as cosmic forces such as Milankovitch cycles, are also determined by organic activity in a myriad of ways exposed in Chapter 2. That is, the molecular composition of the atmosphere, the water cycle, the formation of sedimentary bedrock and, most importantly for capitalist growth, the existence of extractable deposits of hydrocarbons are all the result of biological activity and ecological processes but are subsumed to the temporality of geological processes.
2. Aaron Greenfield and T.E. Graedel, "The Omnivorous Diet of Modern Technology," *Resources, Conservation and Recycling* 74 (2013): 1–7, https://doi.org/10.1016/j.resconrec.2013.02.010.

metabolisms in their diverse forms, have as a limiting factor the capacity to tap into the flows ecological (fast) cycles. Expressed succinctly, societies that primarily have an agrarian metabolic regime depend on ecological cycles and their productivity—through the human appropriation of net primary production (NPP). This biophysical surplus mediates access to elements from geological cycles such as minerals, whether as cut stone, clay or metal ore and to the means of their transformation. In agrarian and hunter-gatherer-forager societies both the extraction and transformation of geological elements depend on human and animal work fed and sustained by the NPP of agricultural activity and extracted NPP inputs such as timber.

In agrarian metabolic regimes, the social organization of the capture and conversion of agricultural, marine and forest NPP is what sustains a given level of human and animal productive activity. As capitalism developed this metabolic structure was inversed: it is by tapping into material stocks produced by slow and long geological cycles that capitalist societies sustain their agricultural production and harvests of biomass. Geology mediates ecology, but at the price of an acceleration of the geological cycles that are mobilized by capitalist metabolism, whether it be the carbon cycle or the dissipation rates of key minerals and metals (a process geologically akin to erosion). The resulting acceleration is experienced as geological change. The socio-ecological consequences of this inversion are immense, for the stability of Earth system processes, as biogeochemical cycles are forced into zones of instability.

From the perspective of capitalist society which completed the transition to fossil and industrial metabolism in the last century, this inversion has been experienced (and celebrated) as an emancipation from the limits of the ecological cycles of the Earth and a prospect of unlimited, open-ended progressive economic growth.[3] Yet this emancipation has proven to be illusory, as limits have shifted from the ecological to the geological, with a mode of historicity—timescale—that challenges the experiential form of social temporality and historicity of modernity.[4] Provoked geological change takes on a catastrophic and crisis form; it

---

3. A penetrating study of the ideological and cultural aspects of this change can be found in Pierre Charbonnier, *Abondance et Liberté, une histoire environnementale des idées politiques*. Paris: La découverte, 2020.
4. Timothy Morton, *Hyperobjects: Philosophy and Ecology after the End of the World*. Minneapolis, MN: University of Minnesota Press, 2013.

sets in motion a catastrophist time horizon as expressed, for example, in the various scenarios of the trajectory of the Earth system presented in IPCCC reports. Historicity takes on a "time running out" form which replaces the modern experience of social time as a vector of progress. In the following chapters we will try and capture the historical specificity of the fossil metabolic regime of capitalist society that has led to this new mode of temporality that could be named the "condition of the Anthropocene."[5]

SOCIO-METABOLIC REGIMES IN HISTORY

The tryptic distinction between hunting-gathering, agrarian and fossil-industrial metabolic regimes, proposed by Sieferle as a way of classifying societies in history resembles many like typologies that have marked social theory in the last two centuries. The specificity of Sieferle's typology is its construction around "the main sources of energy and the main technologies of energy conversion,"[6] which then implies "patterns and levels of resource use, demographic and settlement patterns, patterns of use of human time and labor, institutional characteristics and communication patterns."[7] It is important to note the dialectical nature of the relations between biophysical and socio-cultural factors in this typology. Access to a given source of energy and a given mode of conversion does not "cause" the emergence of given patterns of social practice and structure. As we have argued throughout this book, biophysical and social processes intermediate each other, so windmills might appear inside feudal societies, but they did not lead to the rise of lords and they most certainly existed in a much wider array of social formations, some relatively egalitarian.

---

5. See Jeremy Davies, *The Birth of the Anthropocene*. Oakland, CA: University of California Press, 2018, but also Christophe Bonneil and Jean-Baptiste Fressoz, *The Shock of the Anthropocene: The Earth, History and Us*, trans. David Fernbach. London: Verso, 2016, as well as Andreas Malm, *Fossil Capital: The Rise of Steam Power and the Roots of Global Warming*. London; Verso, 2016.
6. Rolf Peter Sieferle, *The Subterranean Forest: Energy Systems and the Industrial Revolution. Nature in Retrospective: A History of Man and his Environment*. Cambridge: The White Horse Press, 2001.
7. Fridolin Krausmann, Marina Fischer-Kowalski, Heinz Schandl and Nina Eisenmenge, "The Global Sociometabolic Transition: Past and Present Metabolic Profiles and their Future Trajectories," *Journal of Industrial Ecology* 12(5–6) (2008): 639, https://doi.org/10.1111/j.1530-9290.2008.00065.x.

This is furthermore complicated by the fact that the typology of metabolic regimes does not exactly fit the classification of modes of production or economic types common to current critical political economy or social theory.[8] Capitalism as a social form and as an economy can be found on either side of the historical transition from agrarian to fossil-industrial metabolism. The early or pre-fossil capitalist economies were bounded in their development by the constraints of their metabolic base: agrarian capitalism, plantation capitalism and mercantilist capitalism are caught in and limited by the metabolic cycles and surplus of the agrarian metabolic regime. This metabolic base both limits growth and expansion as well as the degree of subsumption of productive and consumptive relations by capitalist processes. Industrial capital, as depicted in Marx's *Capital*, because of its fossil capital metabolic foundations, is characterized on the contrary by perpetual growth, much deeper global geographical expansion and integration of production as well as the real subsumption of productive and consumptive relations by capital. A metabolic rate measures the annual throughput mobilized by a society on a per capita basis (a metric used in Chapter 1). The higher the metabolic rate, the larger the biophysical scale of the economic process necessary for the reproduction of a given society. Here we will use a measure of the metabolic rate calculated by Marina Fischer-Kowalski and Anke Schaffartzik in energy units instead of mass of matter.[9] In this manner, it is possible to characterize the metabolic types according to their energy throughput.

Table 3.1 calculates the metabolic rate by expressing in joules the energy used either directly or indirectly as energy embedded in food, feed and biomass-based raw materials,[10] and compares these rates to a "metabolic base rate" of a human body. Hovering around three gigajoules (GJ) per year per capita, this metabolic base rate includes all endosomatic energy tied to the biological metabolism of an average human to which is added the exosomatic energy needed to cook food with a simple

---

8.   Sieferle does explicitly refer to the Marxian concept of mode of production as a methodological inspiration for his typology; see Sieferle, *The Subterranean Forest*.

9.   Marina Fischer-Kowalski and Anke Schaffartzik, "Energy Availability and Energy Sources as Determinants of Societal Development in a Long-Term Perspective," *MRS Energy & Sustainability—A Review Journal* 2(e1) (February 2015): 1, https://doi.org/10.1557/mre.2015.2.

10.   This corresponds to the category of direct energy consumption.

fire. All joules above and beyond this rate have an "exosomatic" form, meaning they are exteriorized as a nexus of practical activity (provisioning through gathering or harvesting), controlled and directed physical processes mediated by tools (such as heating clay with fire) and eventually working machines (heating a frozen pizza in a microwave). When comparing these rates, one captures the degree or intensity of the social mediation of the biological metabolism of human beings, the expenditure of energy needed to "express in a determined form" a "way of life."

Table 3.1 Socio-metabolic regimes and energy

Regime	Average metabolic rate GJ per capita per year	Factor from basic rate
Basic metabolic rate (including use of fire for food)	3	1
Hunter-gatherer metabolic regime	11	4
Agrarian metabolic regime	50	17
Fossil Industrial	200	66

Source: adapted from Marina Fischer-Kowalski and Anke Schaffartzik, "Energy Availability and Energy Sources as Determinants of Societal Development in a Long-Term Perspective," *MRS Energy & Sustainability—A Review Journal* 2(e1) (February 2015): 1, https://doi.org/10.1557/mre.2015.2.

Hunter-gatherers have a typical metabolic rate that is four times that of their basic bodily rate. This not only represents work such as hunting, gathering, but also burning, cooking, cutting and felling wood, shaping stones and constructing shelters. It also represents energy expended and nature put to work to craft totems, paint figures and practice rituals. Agrarian metabolism typically mobilizes 50GJ per person per annum, a metabolic rate that implies exosomatic work 17 times that of basic endosomatic energy expenditure. This is achieved through the production of agrarian ecosystems which generate net primary production specifically for social uses. Or, put another way, in this regime, endosomatic metabolism and everyday life have come to depend on the exosomatic metabolism materialized in cultivated fields, cleared pastures and managed woodlands. A salient characteristic of agrarian metabolism is its boundedness inside a productive ecological cycle with a metabolic floor and ceiling, giving a periodic form to the secular trend of its metabolic rate through time. With a typical metabolic rate of 200GJ today, up from 85GJ in 1900, fossil-industrial societies have shifted their material base from a process bounded by ecological cycles to one of open-ended growth. This very high metabolic rate, 66 times the basic rate, also expresses the degree of dependence of fossil-industrial societies on exosomatic work performed by machines which replace socialized ecosystems as the locus on which everyday life and the endosomatic metabolism of human beings now depend.

AGRARIAN METABOLISM

The agrarian metabolic regime began in the neolithic period with the development of agriculture and still today defines the mode of existence of a significant proportion of humanity.[11] Its central figure is the peasant community, direct producers of social wealth predominately in the form of grown and extracted biomass. Peasant communities produce and harvest in forms specific to their cultures: this biomass is food for humans, feed and fodder for livestock, fuel, fiber and wood for manufacturing, construction and thermal energy production. Extracted and harvested biomass represents typically at least 95 percent of the material throughput of agrarian societies in mass terms, compared to 26 percent

---

11. Recent archeological and anthropological evidence gathered by Graeber and Wengrow on paleolithic societies goes against a clean cut between hunting-gathering and agricultural societies such as implied in the theory of a neolithic agricultural revolution; see David Graeber and David Wengrow, *The Dawn of Everything: A New History of Humanity*. New York: Farrar, Straus and Giroux, 2021. During the Holocene, most human societies have had an opportunistic and flexible relation to both hunting–gathering and cultivation, all the while developing urban forms of living and sometimes hierarchical social relations based on tributary structures. All these societies were involved in conscious ecological relations that shaped and transformed ecosystems as implied in the concept of colonization including the production of ecologically improbable agro-ecosystems or forest communities. It is only in the recent "late Holocene" period that a minority of societies shifted in a radical manner to an agrarian mode of living in Eurasia and Central and South America. These societies have become demographically dominant and it is the European variant that also saw the emergence of capitalism as a social formation, the ideal type of an agrarian metabolic regime constructed by Sieferle refers primarily to this historical case. This being said, the material gathered by Graeber and Wengrow does show the need to revise the typology of metabolic regimes to take into account the diversity of historical situations during the early and middle Holocene.

in industrial societies today.[12] Peasant communities must not only provide for their reproduction and cultural flourishing—reproduce their mode of living—but they must also produce a surplus of biomass which sustains non-agricultural populations, urban modes of living, as well as communities and social activities of extraction and transformation of non-organic matter. The modalities whereby this surplus is extracted and produced, its size and composition, the proportion that is appropriated by non-producers, the modalities of its distribution and use, all these determinants of the economic process of agrarian societies show enormous variation throughout history and cultures.[13] Our focus here is on the basic structure of the agrarian metabolic regime examined as an ideal type. We have thus abstracted away these variations, although examining specific historical cases would be a necessary endeavor for socio-metabolic analysis in the future.

From a biophysical perspective, the core feature of the agrarian metabolic regime is the development of what Sieferle has called a "controlled solar energy system" or "active solar energy use" primarily through agriculture.[14] Sieferle distinguishes this social control of net primary production from "passive solar energy" use of hunter-gatherer societies. In terms of ecology, agrarian societies:

> begin to control key parameters of ecosystems such as vegetation cover, elements of the water and nutrient cycles, and by this, create colonized areas in which they concentrate solar energy for the photosynthesis of plants they cultivate. [... They] deliberately intervene in the evolution of plants and animals selectively favoring species variants more appropriate for human use and by seeking to eradicate food competitors.[15]

The result is a social metabolism based on the organization of biomass *production* mediated by human and animal work. This contrasts with

---

12.   Fischer-Kowalski and Schaffartzik, Energy Availability and Energy Sources as Determinants of Societal Development in a Long-Term Perspective."
13.   For example, socio-metabolic research has found that in pre-modern Europe the range of non-agricultural to agriculture population was 3 to 10 per 100, a range depending on the degree of exploitation and the productivity of agriculture (Fischer-Kowalski and Schaffartzik 2015).
14.   Sieferle, *The Subterranean Forest*.
15.   Sieferle quoted in Fischer-Kowalski and Schaffartzik, Energy Availability and Energy Sources as Determinants of Societal Development in a Long-Term Perspective," 5.

hunting and gathering which is based on the collection and extraction of pre-existing biomass in ecosystems.[16] The agrarian mode implies both the social production of these novel ecosystems and their active management to generate harvestable biomass, either directly through plants or indirectly through grazing animals. The ecosystems produced to generate this biomass in determined forms can be differentiated along a gradient that measures their distance from the ecological equilibrium that can be considered their "natural" state in a given biome.

At one end, where distance would be maximum, are the intensively cultivated garden plots, orchards or terraced rice paddies and other forms of "wet agriculture"; in a middling range, one finds open fields of non-irrigated cereal crops; closer to equilibrium, there are pastures and then woodlands; and at near equilibrium, are those territories and ecosystems known in medieval Europe as "common wastes, that is, forests, wetlands that are not actively managed."[17] This gradient is one of human and animal work expended and sunk into creating and maintaining the non-equilibrium state of these novel and often improbable ecosystems. The further a socialized agro-ecosystem is from equilibrium: the more work has been sunk into its creation and the more work must be expended to maintain its productivity and generate a yield. But inversely, the more intensely worked a given unit of land of average quality is, the higher the yield, meaning potentially the larger the metabolic surplus. And this can translate into a larger non-agricultural population per unit of land. Further on, we will return to this question of agricultural productivity and the surplus question.

Agrarian societies do extract and transform abiotic materials created by geological forces and cycles, minerals and metals, but at a scale incommensurably small when compared to the metabolic profile of contemporary capitalist societies. Accounting for less than 5 percent of the throughput mass, these materials are nonetheless, especially in the

16. The metabolic structures and relations of hunting-gathering societies did lead to significant ecological change and disruptions, in particular through the use of fire. These societies did favor the dispersal and foster the growth of plants essential to their mode of living, but not on a scale comparable to agrarian and industrial societies.
17. Improved capitalist agriculture, as was developed in England from the seventeenth to the nineteenth century, though dominated by dry field cereal production and pastures, would be closer to wet agriculture on this gradient given the intensification of human and animal labor as well as the nature of the plant communities established in both agro-ecosystems.

case of metals, transformed into tools crucial to the capacity to extract and further transform matter and produce biomass. In terms of energy throughput, the essential mediation of the extraction and transformation of matter in the economic process of agrarian societies are two energy forms: mechanical energy and thermal energy. Though these societies know how to harness and convert the kinetic energy of the wind and running water into mechanical work, the essential input of mechanical work comes from muscle work, mediated by the metabolism of human and animal bodies. Thermal energy, obtained essentially from wood combustion, was not only an everyday means for the transformation of food and a source of heat and light, but it was also an essential means for the transformation of minerals, both metallic and non-metallic (clay) as well as biomass (beer) in quasi-industrial scale processes. Though most agrarian societies used fossil fuels for various purposes, they did not extract and exploit these energy carriers at scales comparable to what we will see in the fossil-industrial metabolic regime of capitalism. To illustrate this, let us examine England on the verge of the Industrial Revolution in 1700. In this, "advanced organic economy," human labor, animal work and firewood accounted for 80 percent of per capita energy consumption in almost equal shares, coal already accounted for 18 percent of per capita energy consumption and wind and water made up for the remaining 2 percent.[18] Corporeal work, as well the harvest of annual growth of biomass in the form of trees, by far dominated as the core mediation of the metabolic process of these societies. And one must not forget that the access to thermal energy carriers, such as firewood and coal, was essentially mediated by the mechanical work expended by laboring and working bodies: animals and humans in forests, mines and collieries. It is this same labor and work applied to improbable ecosystems in fields, orchards and gardens and to a lesser extent pastures, working with nature that produced the biomass necessary to fuel bodily work. So, if on the one hand the throughput consists essentially of produced biomass, and on the other hand a significant amount of this biomass is converted by laboring bodies into mechanical work, this is, with the ecological process whereby plants produce biomass (nature's work), the central mediation of the economic process of agrarian societies. Surplus, in its most basic

18. E.A. Wrigley, *Energy and the English Industrial Revolution*. Cambridge: Cambridge University Press, 2010, 94.

form, appears as a quantum of produced and harvested biomass, above and beyond what is needed to reproduce the community of agricultural producers.

THE "PHYSIOCRATIC" STRUCTURE OF THE AGRARIAN METABOLIC REGIME

Figure 3.1 illustrates the constraints and structural relations of agrarian metabolism in a general and ahistorical manner.[19] It is presented here as a conceptual tool with the purpose of highlighting through contrast the historical and ecological specificity of the fossil-based metabolic regime of capital, which will be presented further on. It is built as a two-sector model:[20] on the one hand, a biophysical surplus *production* sector, around socially controlled NPP extracted from an agrarian metabolic cycle; and a biophysical surplus *absorption* sector consisting of non-agricultural social relations of extraction, production, consumption and dissipation.

On the left side of Figure 3.1, one finds the metabolic cycle of agrarian societies: an agricultural population of humans and animals has a defined quantity and quality of labor power that can be expended toward agricultural production and biomass extraction (from forests and bodies of water) through land use. Land use here refers to the colonization and creation of novel socialized ecosystems and their management to generate NPP with "nature's work" existing as an autonomous ecological cycle. This results in a biomass-based social product that sustains both the agricultural and non-agricultural populations. The partition of the social product between these social groups depends on a diversity of social relations of distribution from reciprocity to tributary extraction to market exchange;[21] it does not a priori imply exploitation, though often this has been the case. The analysis of each of these compo-

---

19. Figure 3.1 is inspired by Krausmann et al., "The Global Sociometabolic Transition."
20. It is thus also similar to the model that underlies Wrigley's work on "organic economies" that he has constructed in a dialogue with classical economists, primarily Smith, Malthus and Ricardo. Formally one could qualify this model as physiocratic, given its proximity with Quesnay's "Tableau économique." On Quesnay, see Paul Burkett, "The Value Problem in Ecological Economics: Lessons from the Physiocrats and Marx," *Organization & Environment* 16(2) (2003): 137–167, https://doi.org/10.11 77/1086026603016002001.
21. This latter form is by far the most marginal of the three.

nents of the metabolic cycle could be further refined, for example, the mode of existence of "labor power" varies dramatically from one social form to another: between, for example, a free peasantry, bonded serfs, waged agricultural laborers and chattel slaves. A distinct characteristic of labor power in societies with an agrarian metabolism is the importance of animals which multiplied considerably the amount of work that can be mobilized as well as the power of each unit of labor mobilized by society.[22] One estimate for Europe in 1750 calculates that the "38 million working animals" provided each European with double the work "that could be exerted by his or her body alone."[23] Modes of tenure and ecological organization of land also vary, from common wastes and open fields to enclosed and improved pastures and crop fields to private plantations. Produced and extracted biomass also has variegated modes of existence as social wealth, sometimes presenting itself as an appropriable quantitative mass differentiated according to use and practice, sometimes presenting itself as non-appropriable because it is entirely caught up in reciprocal and care relations. Finally, the agricultural population itself is structured according to social relations of kinship, power and status. But the defining feature of the metabolic cycle is its dual mediation by labor and nature's work in the form of socially oriented ecological productivity. Laboring bodies through their own metabolic activity are, with nature, the dynamic and active elements of this cycle.

On the right side of Figure 3.1, one finds a vertical structure that illustrates the relations of the non-agricultural population to this metabolic cycle, a dependence of this group on the extraction of surplus from this cycle. Yet it contributes to this cycle through the social division of labor by the production and improvement of agricultural and extractive tools and technologies and by the colonization of new land through the development of infrastructures of communication, transport and conquest.

The relation between the sectors of an agrarian is regulated by two limits or constraints—a surplus limit and a transport limit. Both will be superseded by the development of a capitalist fossil metabolic regime; more specifically, it is the way these limits will be superseded that will

---

22. The problem of power will be examined in Chapter 4 as its exponential growth is a defining feature of the fossil-industrial metabolic regime of capitalism.

23. Astrid Kander, Paolo Malanima and Paul Warde, *Power to the People: Energy in Europe Over the Last Five Centuries*. Princeton, NJ: Princeton University Press, 2013, 75.

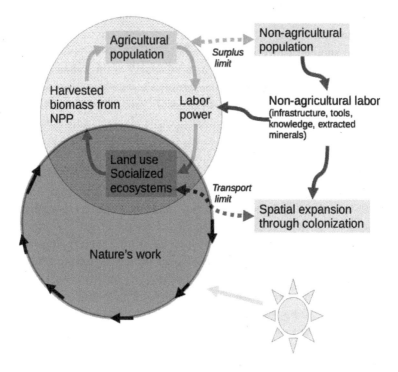

Figure 3.1   Agrarian metabolic cycle

Source: Inspired by Fridolin Krausmann, Marina Fischer-Kowalski, Heinz Schandl and
Nina Eisenmenge, "The Global Sociometabolic Transition: Past and Present Metabolic
Profiles and their Future Trajectories," *Journal of Industrial Ecology* 12(5–6) (2008):
637–656, https://doi.org/10.1111/j.1530-9290.2008.00065.x.

lay the basis for the growth pattern typical of this new metabolic regime.
The latter refers to the limited capacity to transport the biomass on which
rests the metabolism of agrarian societies. Overland transport of biomass
is limited by the energy demand of the bodies—animal and human—who
must haul, cart and carry the social products to centers of non-agricultural population such as cities. At one point, the energy consumed by
the carriers equals the energy content of what is hauled and this structures and limits urban and hinterland relations. This limit can be partly
overcome by water travel but, as one moves away from riverbanks and
coastlines, the capacity to keep a massive quantum of biomass in circulation dwindles rapidly. The surplus limit has much deeper implications.

THE DUAL NATURE OF THE AGRARIAN SURPLUS AND ITS LIMITS

The surplus constraint faced by agrarian societies takes on two forms. A first constraint is access to an extractable biophysical surplus and the capacity to convert this biophysical surplus into useful work by laboring bodies. A second constraint is the capacity to extract from this biophysical surplus a social surplus, either in the form of non-agricultural work or appropriated biomass by non-agricultural populations. The first constraint is ecological. Like any life form, humans depend on a trophic web based on net primary production by plants. Agricultural activity implies creating ecosystems able to produce enough biomass to ensure the reproduction of the direct producers and those that labor and work in the fields be they human or animal, ensure the production of enough seed to resow cultivated fields, in a sense, ensure the reproduction of the agro-ecosystem itself as specific plant community. If NPP falls below this level, then agrarian societies face the prospect of collapse, seed must be eaten, agro-ecosystems evolve toward a natural equilibrium because they are not maintained through sunk labor and work. Typically, the biophysical surplus that is sought from agricultural activity is larger than what is strictly needed to ensure the reproduction of the direct producers. It can also sustain a non-agricultural population and non-agricultural forms of labor. This can be further modulated by the intensity of work applied to each unit of land. As mentioned earlier, applying more work per unit of land is also a means of generating a larger surplus, inside the metabolic limits of laboring bodies of course. Because of this limit of individual laboring bodies, the capacity to intensify labor expended and sunk per unit of land requires growth of the agricultural population. Yet more hands in the fields also means more mouths at the table. Intensified agricultural production, in the terms laid out above, also means an agro-ecosystem further from equilibrium, more fragile and less able to reproduce itself through its own ecological relations, needing constant inputs of labor and work to exist. And as both Malthus and Ricardo theorized, a point can be reached where the contribution of a new hand is less than what is required to feed the mouth that comes with it, given the limited quantity of optimally fertile land. At this point, the agricultural regime reaches a metabolic limit; this idea, theorized as Malthusian cycles, was central to the worldview of classical economists.

85

So, what can be appropriated as a social surplus depends on the capacity to generate a biophysical surplus through socio-ecological relations and labor. And this biophysical surplus is limited by the capacity to enhance the biological productivity of agro-ecosystems, which depends not only on social factors such as demographics, but also on knowledge, tools, domesticated life forms, and ecological factors such as soil fertility, climate and interactions with other livings beings such as insects, weeds and fungi. These are the ecological parameters that agrarian societies attempt to control, not necessarily to maximize the size of the agrarian surplus, but to reach a level of production of harvestable biomass that ensures the reproduction of their social structures, including a sophisticated social division of labor with a potentially important fraction of non-agricultural laborers, as well as structures of domination and exploitation.[24] This non-agricultural population contributes indirectly to the productivity of biomass production through "improvement," in particular by the artisanal stratum able to design and construct agricultural tools (such as metal plows and scythes).

---

24. Agrarian capitalism which developed in England on the contrary contains the normative constraints that spur the development of social relations of production, which will push landlords and capitalist farmers to maximize biomass surplus production through intensified agricultural practices. Furthermore, the form of this surplus is appropriable as a commodity. This unique historical process led to the development of an "advanced organic economy" that sustained through agricultural productivity gains a proportion of non-agricultural—urban population unheard of in agrarian societies and prepared the transition to industrial capitalism and its fossil-metabolic regime. Wrigley, who coined the expression "advanced organic economy," enumerates a number of factors other than the transition to capitalist class relations of production and property in the countryside; see E.A. Wrigley, *Energy and the English Industrial Revolution.* Cambridge: Cambridge University Press, 2010. Wood, following Brenner, insists on the latter forces as decisive factors; see Ellen Meiksins Wood, *Empire of Capital.* London: Verso, 2005. Commenting on this debate is outside of the scope of this work, but it would be interesting to revisit the transition question from within the metabolic perspective presented here. Finally, with Bellamy Foster, one could argue that the immense productivity gains of capitalist agriculture which grew the surplus were, in the long run, ecologically unsustainable and led to a series of metabolic rifts in soil nutrient cycles and could only be maintained with the constant input of extracted minerals appropriated in colonial relations of appropriation, or what Jason Moore has analyzed as metabolic "shifts." See Jason W. Moore, "The Value of Everything? Work, Capital, and Historical Nature in the Capitalist World-Ecology," *Review* 37(3–4) (2014): 245–292; and Jason W. Moore, *Capitalism in the Web of Life: Ecology and the Accumulation of Capital.* New York: Verso, 2015.

Social appropriation and distribution of the surplus is often mediated by relations of domination and violence of one social group on another, but this need not be the case. Egalitarian societies also historically generated metabolic surpluses. This process of appropriation led to the development of symbolic instruments capable of representing produced biomass as an abstract quantum of appropriable social wealth. Concretely, this materialized in systems of weights and measures as well as standard quantitative units to count staple foods such as grain. Grains in many civilizations became units of account for bureaucracies and hierarchies that dominated peasant producers through tributary relations of appropriation. Other typical means by which biomass could be objectified as social wealth and absorbed into circuits of distribution, which included non-agricultural populations, were systems of reciprocity and relations of market exchange explored by Karl Polanyi.[25] While the latter are central features of agrarian societies and often reflected a non-hierarchical basic communism (Graeber)[26] governed by an imperative of the irreducible minimum (Bookchin),[27] market-type exchange relations, whether monetized or not, were exceptions until the advent of capitalism.[28]

CONCLUSION ON SURPLUS AND AGRARIAN METABOLISM

Exploring the social metabolism of agrarian societies, the diversity of socio-ecological arrangements and niches, the complexity of the relations between production, reproduction and the division of labor, should and could fill the pages of scores of volumes. In this short and modest chapter, we have delineated an abstract and general model which focused on the socio-ecological relations of this form of metabolism, its constraints and limits, and what this implies for a theory of the metabolic and economic surplus.

25.   Karl Polanyi, *The Great Transformation: The Political and Economic Origins of Our Time*. Boston, MA: Beacon Press, (1944) 2011.
26.   David Graeber, *Debt: The First 5,000 Years*. New York: Melville House, 2012.
27.   Murray Bookchin, *Ecology of Freedom: The Emergence and Dissolution of Hierarchy*. Palo Alto, CA: Cheshire Books, 1982.
28.   Some urban centers of traditional agrarian societies did undergo periods of intense commercialization, such as Rome and the Song imperial China. See Ting Chen and James Kai-Sing Kung, "Commercial Revolution in Medieval China," August 21, 2022, SSRN: https://ssrn.com/abstract=3960074.

In an abstract and formal sense, we can characterize the economic surplus in the agrarian regime as biomass that must be produced—ex post—above and beyond what is needed to ensure the subsistence of the direct producers and reproduce their socio-ecological conditions of production. Producers here include both laboring humans and the animals they exploit. Furthermore, the expended and sunk labor and work of these humans and animals is obtained from their own metabolic activity, as implied in the concept of metabolic cycle presented above. The work they achieve is a direct outcome of the biomass their bodies metabolize. Once generated, this surplus can be directed to the reproduction of non-agricultural classes which, throughout most of history, remain a narrow minority. From a socio-historical perspective, this surplus production did not focus on generating a growing mass of matter in the abstract—such as implied in the throughput concept examined earlier—or of energy which can be objectified in units such as joules as we saw in Chapter 2, but on the constraint to generate appropriable *concrete* forms of material wealth in the context of tributary relations of exploitation and to a lesser and more marginal extent market relations of exchange. It is also this surplus which is the condition of possibility for the access to other segments of the material throughput in agrarian societies, in particular those critical elements of geological origin such as metals. And the capacity to transform these elements into use-values also rests on the surplus extracted from the agrarian metabolic cycle which sustains non-agricultural producers. The larger the produced surplus, the deeper the social division of labor in agrarian metabolic regimes, the more this labor can contribute to raising agro-ecological productivity. Though enhanced productivity is often not a desired and sought-after objective of agrarian producers, this process has a defined ecological ceiling where productivity is biophysically bounded.

Surplus typical of the fossil regimes we are about to study have an inverse mode of existence. Fossil energy regimes find before themselves pre-existing stocks of useful energy they can mobilize and dispose of once they have been extracted. The surplus exists; the problem is its extraction and then its consumption. It is this pre-existing stock of exergy that mediates labor and more generally relations of production, including the production of biomass. In this inverted world, it is the combustion of elements of geological origin that are a condition of possibility for the capacity to labor in industry and as well in agriculture. The metabolic foundation of society shifts from ecology to geology and on this base capitalism finds the material mediation of the spectacular and hubristic growth that has characterized its development in the last two centuries and a half.

4

Fossil-Based Industrial Metabolism

We began our study of metabolic regimes with the remark that categories such as energy and matter in an abstract modern and scientific sense are not effective symbolic and instituted mediations of the economic process of *all* societies. "The idea that heat, work and light could be summarized under the common term 'energy,' or that water, wind, motion and nourishment could be the same in some way, was alien to agrarian society," remarks Sieferle. Adding that: "Only within the framework of the industrial system did a complete conversion of different energy forms become possible, and only then could the general term 'energy' arrive."[1] The modern concept of energy expresses the historical emancipation and abstraction of "the capacity to do work" from its embodiment in the determined and incommensurable forms that characterized agrarian societies: laboring humans and working animals, and also water flows, waterfalls, sunlight and wind gusts,[2] which were the prime movers before industrial fossil metabolism. This movement of abstraction was both an intellectual endeavor in the form of the theory of thermodynamics, as well as a material practice through the systematic development of "energized artifacts," the most significant being the coal fired steam engine.[3]

When studying agrarian societies from a metabolic perspective, the analysis and calculus of energy flows such as "primary energy consumption" implies applying to these societies a methodological device outside of their system of representations, social relations and structures.

---

1.   Rolfe Peter Sieferle, *The Subterranean Forest: Energy Systems and the Industrial Revolution*. Cambridge: The White Horse Press, 2001, 19–20.

2.   Larry Lohmann and Nicholas Hildyard, *Energy, Work and Finance*. Sturminster Newton: The Corner House, 2014.

3.   François Vatin, *Le travail, économie et physique, 1780–1830*. Paris: Presses universitaires de France, 1993; and more recently Cara Daggett, *The Birth of Energy: Fossil Fuels, Thermodynamics, and the Politics of Work*. Durham, NC: Duke University Press, 2019.

Energy is not a social mediation in these societies, though it remains a biophysical determination of social practice and reality. This outside-ness disappears entirely in the case of those societies with a fossil-based industrial metabolism, a metric such as "primary energy consumption" captures an internal and reflexively developed throughput driver. These societies actively strive to develop energy flows as such and the same can be said for extracted material flows. Growing these flows has meant pur-posefully breaking through the barriers to limitless expansion inherent to the agrarian regime.

BREAKING OUT OF THE STRUCTURAL LIMITS OF AGRARIAN METABOLISM

In Chapter 3, we identified two structural limits to the material expansion of the agrarian metabolic regime: a surplus constraint and a transport constraint. By shifting the basis of the production of the biophysi-cal surplus from ecologically determined flows to geologically formed stocks it was possible for a new fossil-industrial regime to enter into a long phase of exponential growth of both output, throughput and urban population. The causes of this growth will be examined in the context of the institutional analysis of capitalist social relations, but the extraction of mineral stocks of fossils fuels and of metal ores was an enabling and necessary condition. Coal, of course, is the initial and core extracted resource on which the biophysical surplus is based in this new regime. Other fossil fuels followed rapidly and contributed to the growth rate of primary energy consumption during the whole twentieth century and most intensely during its latter half—a period some environmental his-torians have dubbed the Great Acceleration.[4] As shown in Table 4.1, the metabolic imperative faced by an agrarian regime is to produce a surplus by growing biomass, while the metabolic imperative of the fossil regime is to extract and burn as efficiently as possible a fossil-fuel surplus. This distinction can be captured by what we can call "Wrigley's metabolic rule of growth":[5]

---

4. John Robert McNeill, Peter O. Engelke and Peter Engelke, *The Great Acceleration: An Environmental History of the Anthropocene Since 1945*. Cambridge, MA: Belknap Press of Harvard University Press, 2014.
5. I use the expression "rule" in contrast to "law" to highlight the fact that I consider this to be a factual observation that does not identify causal mechanisms. The laws—or

The marginal cost of production must rise in an organic economy beyond a certain level of output. In contrast, in energy rich, mineral based economies it normally fell with increasing output. Increased output did not make further progress more difficult but rather the reverse. Falling production costs encouraged rapid growth in demand, and a virtuous circle became established.[6]

By applying the surplus to further surplus extraction of stocks of fossil fuels, the regime develops a capacity of continuous growth and emancipates itself from an immediate dependance on ecological cycles.[7] By using the work of fossil fuels to transform on a mass and systematic scale other mineral resources such as metallic ores, industry also breaks with its dependance on extraction and production mediated and limited by a flow of energy and materials from ecological cycles, such as transforming trees into charcoal to smelt iron, or transforming grain into embodied muscle power to mine ore through human labor and animal work. These materials and new energy sources were then recursively applied to extractive activities, further intensifying the extractive flow of fossil fuels and materials critical to the development of this metabolic regime such as iron and steel. This recursiveness, where fossil fuels and metal work alongside human labor and *multiply* labor power to extract more fossil fuels and minerals, is a core feature of fossil-industrial metabolism.

For some social ecologists, the beginnings of the fossil-industrial metabolic regime are to be found in sixteenth-century Netherlands and the United Kingdom. There and then, according to Marina Fischer-Kowalski, began the "fossil fuel energy subsidy to humanity," through the incorpo-

rather socio-ecological determinations—behind these rules cannot be formulated in the abstract language of Ricardian economics since they are specific to capitalist social relations. For an extensive discussion and critique of the Ricardian and Malthusian models of transition from agrarian to fossil-industrial metabolism where growth is posited as a natural property of social systems, see Andreas Malm, *Fossil Capital: The Rise of Steam Power and the Roots of Global Warming*. London: Verso, 2016, Chapter 12 in particular.

6.   E.A. Wrigley, *Energy and the English Industrial Revolution*. Cambridge: Cambridge University Press, 2010, 195.

7.   The key word here is, of course, immediate. Tapping into geological cycles means contributing to their motion, if this is done on a small scale, the effects will be innocuous, but since growth implies scaling up the process, the impact on the carbon cycle is of geological proportions both in scope and in timescale and already has had dire ecological consequences.

ration of coal and peat into social metabolism on a mass scale.[8] Coal, on the eve of the Industrial Revolution, in the early eighteenth century, did account for 20 percent of the United Kingdom's primary energy supply,[9] and yet it would be a mistake to consider coal use as a heat source as a decisive development that sealed the transition from an agrarian biomass-based to a fossil-fuel-based regime. It is rather when coal was put to work to extract more coal, that one can consider that a transition to a new metabolic regime had commenced. It was a rather banal undertaking, combustion of coal generated heat which was converted via steam into mechanical work through the Newcomen engine which drove a pump. This pump was then used to draw water out of ever-deeper mining shafts and thus transformed inaccessible coal seams into accessible seams.[10] But this banality hides a further core feature of this metabolic regime: the recursive application of extracted energy and matter to extractive activity *grows* the stock of accessible sources of matter and energy: Wrigley's rule in action. In a capitalist society, this recursive application will take the form of capitalized extractive artifacts and capitalized sites of extraction through investment, or accumulation at the "point of extraction."

The second structural constraint that the fossil-fuel regime overcame was the transport limit that agrarian societies faced. Though they had developed sophisticated means of water travel, whether by canal, river or sea, land travel had always been a limiting factor for the expansion of their economic relations and for the development of a deep division of labor, implying an important non-agricultural population. It was possible for luxury goods to circulate widely and globally, but unless waterborne, bulky staple goods such as grain, timber and other construction materials had a limited area of circulation. Railroads, which combined coal-fired steam engines and steel transport infrastructure was one initial way this constraint was surpassed, followed quickly by steamboats and eventually road, air transport and containerized transport—all powered by fossil fuels and built from geological stocks of metals and plastics. These

8. Marina Fischer-Kowalski et al., "A Sociometabolic Reading of the Anthropocene: Modes of Subsistence, Population Size and Human Impact on Earth," *Anthropocene Review* 1(1) (2014): 15.
9. Fischer-Kowalski et al., "A Sociometabolic Reading of the Anthropocene," 15.
10. The same logic has been applied to oil and gas in the twenty-first century, capitalization of extraction has led to the development of "unconventional methods," which have grown accessible reserves hydrocarbons.

new means of circulation were essential to the development of the mass flows of staple goods, primary materials and people, that have marked the development of capitalism in the last 150 years. Five economic consequences are notable, which we have termed "Bunker effects," since they are adapted from Stephen Bunker's work on extractive accumulation:[11]

1. The new fossil-fuel-powered means of circulation where the basis for an upscaling of the volume of extracted matter in circulation, and thus upscaling extraction, as well as the cheapening of transport and end-user costs, which contributed to the mass adoption of these materials in the metabolism of industrial societies. This demand contributed to the formation of a supply regime of standardized grades of extracted materials, serializing the biophysical throughput.

2. The accumulation and use of these new means of circulation contributed significantly to the demand for the very materials that marked the transition to the new industrial metabolism, metals and fossil fuels in particular where crucial materials for the development of railroads and then other means of transport such as shipping. Mineral aggregates were also massively needed for road building.

3. The development of means of circulation profoundly transformed the division of labor both inside societies and between them, spurring the development of long circuits for the basic and bulky materials of industrial metabolism, sustaining mass extraction and mass adoption of these materials not only in the advanced capitalist core but also in the world over. The diversity that characterizes the materiality of artifacts and infrastructures in agrarian societies has been gradually erased by the homogenizing effect of the mass flows of plastic, particle board, concrete and basic metals.[12]

---

11. All five consequences are also tied to Wrigley's rule of growth presented earlier. See Stephen G. Bunker, "How Ecologically Uneven Developments Put the Spin on the Treadmill of Production," *Organization & Environment* 18(1) (2005): 38–54, https://doi.org/10.1177/1086026604270043.

12. Behind the apparent homogeneity of mass flows and of the form of material stocks is a global division of labor that has rested on the development of the heterogeneity of the socio-economic and ecological conditions of extraction and transformation of these materials. Power asymmetries between core and peripheries, and between global corporations and local communities and economies are the dominant social forces

4. The development of long circuits also impacts the circulation of intermediary and final goods and has been the basis for the geographic separation between point of extraction, point of production, point of consumption and point of dissipation, as well as the more recent spatial fragmentation of production through the development of complex commodity chains and circuits of intermediary goods—circuits controlled by large multinational monopolistic corporations that actively manage these commodity chains.

5. The new means of mass circulation are also crucial to modern forms of urbanization and suburbanization; not only have they changed the morphology of cities and the possibilities of mobility of people and matter, but they have also profoundly transformed urban–hinterland relations, metabolically detaching global cities from their immediate rural surroundings and embedding them in global flows of matter and energy. This has then forced rural economies to adapt their metabolism and productive activities to the generation of flows of massified and serialized commodities at a global scale or worst as sinks able to absorb mass flows of waste.

Having broken through the barriers that limited the material expansion of the agrarian regime, fossil-industrial metabolism exponentially grew the scale of its energy and matter throughput flows and thus its capacity to generate and accumulate material stocks. Table 4.1 summarizes the salient features of this metabolic regime through a comparison with the agrarian regime we have studied in Chapter 3.

GROWTH, SCALE AND SUBSTANCE OF FOSSIL-BASED INDUSTRIAL METABOLISM

As we have seen already in Chapter 3, the scale of fossil metabolism, when measured by metabolic rate for energy or matter, is three to five times larger than the metabolism of agrarian societies (these values are copied in column 1 of Table 4.1). But as shown in the Figures 4.1 and 4.2, another

---

that have shaped the unequal geographies of global material flows from source to sink throughout the existence of this regime. This has been systematically explored by Alf Hornborg in his various works on unequal ecological exchange.

Table 4.1   Salient features of agrarian and fossil-industrial metabolism

Regime and metabolic rate for energy and material use (per capita, per year)	Main energy form	Development pattern	Surplus form and constraint	Dominant form of work	Biophysical mediation
Agrarian *40–70 GJ* *3–6 T*	Grain and biomass	Cyclical, base and ceiling, diminishing returns	Produced biomass, plant and generate the surplus	Human and animal metabolism sustains labor power	Ecological relations
Fossil-industrial *150–400 GJ* *15–25 T* 3 to 5 times larger than agrarian regime	Fossil fuels	Growth, continuous rising returns	Fossilized biomass, extract and burn the surplus	Prime mover mediates human labor	Geological relations

salient feature of this regime is *growth*.[13] These figures present the best available estimates of the global throughput growth during the last 150 to 200 years; Figure 4.1 focuses on energy throughput while Figure 4.2 focuses on material flows.

A first commonality is their growth pattern. Throughput growth has two distinct phases: an initial phase where growth took on linear form during the nineteenth century and into the early twentieth century, with an inflection point reached in the 1950s, when growth took on an exponential form. The first phase corresponds to the Industrial Revolution and its transformative impact on the economic process; the second phase corresponds to the epochal phenomenon of the Great Acceleration. A second commonality is the relative decline in importance of biomass flows (whether accounted for as an energy source or as a material flow) in the overall metabolic profile of human societies during this period. In agrarian regimes (including capitalist ones), biomass typically provides at least 95 percent of societal energy needs. The same can be said of biomass-based artifacts typical of agrarian regimes made from wood and

13. And this growth cannot be solely attributed to demographic factors. The data we have on per capita (onshore) energy use for England and Wales in the nineteenth century by Paul Warde shows a rise from 53GJ/capita to 150GJ/capita in 1900; see Astrid Kander, Paolo Malanima and Paul Warde, *Power to the People: Energy in Europe Over the Last Five Centuries*. Princeton, NJ: Princeton University Press, 2013.

natural fibers which were displaced by metal, mineral and hydrocarbon-based materials such as plastics, aluminum and cement.[14] The key word here is *relative*, biomass flows, whether accounted for as energy carriers or as matter, continue to grow in scale throughout the whole history of the regime, but they shift from being all encompassing, to a flow among others.

Figure 4.1 presents an estimate of global primary energy consumption from 1800 to 2020 based on data from Vaclav Smil and the BP annual review of world energy.[15] Counted in terawatts of primary energy, it offers a broad overview of the energy flows that were put to work during the history of the fossil-industrial regime. A first look confirms the two-phased pattern of growth outlined in the paragraph earlier and confirms the relative decline of biomass as an energy carrier. It also belies the common representation of the history of energy use in modern societies as a series of "transitions" based on "substitutions." Rather, we are confronted with a dynamic more aptly described by the concept of energy "additions."[16] As the fossil-industrial regime grew and spread across the globe, engulfing evermore swathes of humanity, new energy sources massively of fossil origin were integrated into the social metabolism on top of existing carriers and they all grew in absolute terms. Coal was the dominant energy carrier up until the 1950s, but its use continued to grow throughout the Great Acceleration and, as of 2019, still accounts for 25 percent of global primary energy consumption. Overall, in 2019, fossil fuels accounted for 78 percent of primary energy consumption, with gas at 23 percent and oil at 31 percent.

Another important feature is the coincidence of the entry into the historical phase, known as the Great Acceleration, with the rapid incorporation of oil into the metabolism of modern societies. In the 1920s, oil represented a mere 5 percent of overall primary energy consumption; a decade later, in 1930, it represented 9 percent. From 1950 to 1970, oil rose

14.   These can be considered forms of abstract materiality akin to the forms of abstract energy outlined earlier.

15.   See Hannah Ritchie, "How have the World's Energy Sources Changed over the Last Two Centuries?" *Our World in Data*, December 1, 2021, https://ourworldindata.org/global-energy-200-years.

16.   Richard York and Shannon Elizabeth Bell, "Energy Transitions or Additions? Why a Transition from Fossil Fuels Requires More Than the Growth of Renewable Energy," *Energy Research & Social Science* 51 (2019): 40–43, https://doi.org/10.1016/j.erss.2019.01.008.

from 19 percent to 40 percent of overall primary energy consumption. The same growth pattern is currently shaping the integration of fossil gas in the global energetic metabolism of societies. Since the 1970s, gas extraction and use as an energy source has been following a pattern of growth similar to that of oil during the twentieth century. This also belies the notion that fossil gas is a transition fuel in the path toward carbon neutral energy systems. Its growth is tied to material transformations that have been locked in during the last five decades by gas dependent processes and artifacts in industry, power generation and buildings.

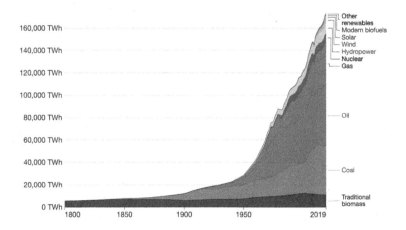

Figure 4.1   Global primary energy consumption by source, 1800–2020

Source: Hannah Ritchie, "How have the World's Energy Sources Changed over the Last Two Centuries?" *Our World in Data*, December 1, 2021, https://ourworldindata.org/global-energy-200-years.

Material flows show the same growth pattern. Figure 4.2 captures throughput growth from 1900 to 2015 and, as with energy flows, a clear inflection point is visible in 1950, with the growth pattern shifting from linear to exponential growth.

Whereas ecologically produced biomass flows still dominate massively at a global level before 1950, afterwards geologically extracted flows (metals, minerals, fossil energy carriers) progressively become dominant: in 1900, the share of biomass in the global throughput was 72 percent; by 1955, this share had dwindled to 50 percent; in 1970, it was 37 percent; and in 2015, it was down to 26 percent. Most importantly, this is not due to a shrinking amount of biomass harvest, but rather to the exponen-

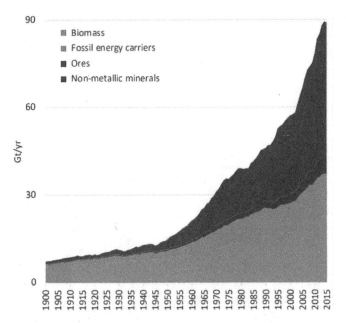

Figure 4.2   Global material extraction, 1900–2015

Source: Fridolin Krausmann, Christian Lauk, Willi Haas and Dominik Wiedenhofer, "From Resource Extraction to Outflows of Wastes and Emissions: The Socioeconomic Metabolism of the Global Economy, 1900–2015," *Global Environmental Change* 52 (September 2018): 131–140, https://doi.org/10.1016/j.gloenvcha.2018.07.003.

tial growth of the extraction of geological stocks. Of these stocks, those necessary to produce cement, as well as aggregates for infill and backfill, attain 50 percent of the throughput mass in the early twenty-first century, up from 23 percent in 1950 and 12 percent in 1900.

Figure 4.3 examines the evolution of the throughput mass during the twentieth century according to the end-use of the materials extracted and in relative terms. From this perspective, the greatest change in the mass throughput is the substitution of the flow of feed by the flow directed toward the manufacture of material artifacts. How do we interpret this collapse of animal feed in the metabolic profile of fossil-industrial societies? Societies did not cease to eat meat during the twentieth century; on the contrary, meat consumption has grown during the Great Acceleration. What did change was the relative marginalization of animal work in the economic process on the one hand, and on the other hand—something that was already apparent in Chapter 1—the growing importance of stock building materials in the throughput, which rose from 17 percent in 1900 to 53 percent in 2015. The proportion of most other flows have remained constant or show slight variations: food diminished slightly; mine tailings have risen in importance; in 2015 the food represented a flow of 4.3Gt per year, while mine tailings represented a flow of 4.8Gt. It is interesting and telling to note that, as societies advance into the Great Acceleration, the mass flow of mine tailings surpasses the mass flow of food![17]

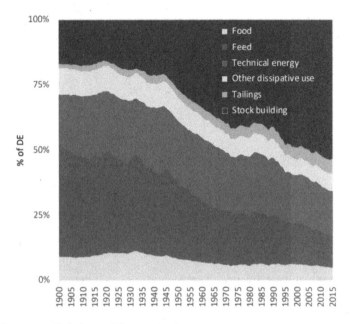

Figure 4.3   Global material extraction by use type, 1900–2015

Source: Krausmann et al., "From Resource Extraction to Outflows of Wastes and Emissions."

Based on the same data set as Figure 4.2, Figure 4.3 estimates global processed outputs, or what we have termed dissipation, for the period 1900 to 2015. Mass dissipation and waste show the same distinctive pattern of growth, with a kink in 1950 and exponential growth afterwards. Unsurprisingly, emissions rapidly become the dominant waste/dissipative form of matter in this metabolic regime, and end of life and

17.   According to the data in Krausmann, it is in 2012 that tailings overtake food; Krausmann et al., "From Resource Extraction to Outflows of Wastes and Emissions."

processing wastes also show a strong and distinctive growth consistent with the type of economic relations we will study in the next chapters.

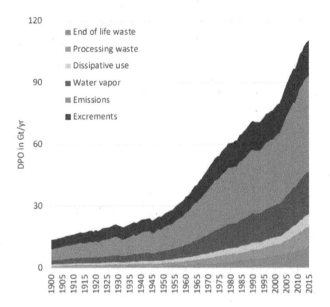

Figure 4.4   Domestic Processed Output (DPO), 1900–2015
Source: Krausmann et al., "From Resource Extraction to Outflows of Wastes and Emissions."

Finally, as we have already seen in Chapter 1, the current metabolic regime is built around the mass combustion of fossil fuels and the mass accumulation of stocks, mainly artifacts. Figures 4.5 and 4.6 present two complimentary outlooks on the accumulation process for the period from 1900 to 2015: Figure 4.5 presents the additions to stocks, whereas Figure 4.6 estimates the mass of accumulated stocks.

Additions to stocks built of concrete and implying infill or other aggregate use predominate in the metabolic profile, but artifacts built out of other materials equally show rapid growth and accumulation after 1950. The dynamics of concrete and cement accumulation have a distinctive pattern that needs explanation. Uses of concrete are self-evident: built structures and infrastructures, the material foundation of urbanization during the last century as well as the materialization of the transport infrastructures such as roads, seaports and airports that linked together these urban environments. The growth pattern of this material can be

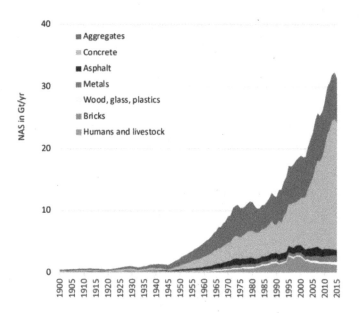

Figure 4.5 Net additions to stock, 1900–2015
Source: Krausmann et al., "From Resource Extraction to Outflows of Wastes and Emissions."

cut into three phases: 1900–1950 where growth was linear; 1950–1995 where cement imposed itself as the prime construction material and was accumulated in urban and industrial environments; and a phase of exponential growth after 1995 tied primarily to the modernization of China and its great transition from an agrarian to a fossil metabolic regime, or what social ecologists have termed the "second great acceleration." In 2017, China accounted for more than 50 percent of the world production of cement; the next largest producer was India. This is then reflected in the mass of accumulated stocks in Figure 4.6.

What these mass-based measures of the throughput growth do not capture—in terms of composition—is the integration of materials not as bulky as cement and aggregates but that are both ecologically and metabolically significant in the fossil-industrial regime. One particularly important case is plastics. In strictly accounting terms, plastics are captured by the metrics that measure fossil-fuel flows, but this obscures the explosion in plastic throughput during the Great Acceleration. According to data compiled by Roland Geyer and colleagues, plastic

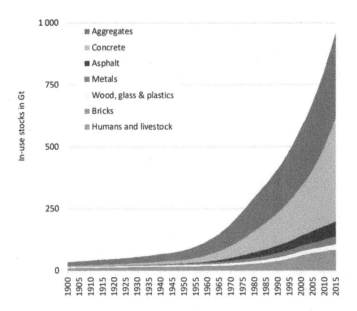

Figure 4.6 In-use stocks of materials, 1900–2015

Source: Krausmann et al., "From Resource Extraction to Outflows of Wastes and Emissions."

production increased from 2MT in 1950 to 380MT in 2015.[18] Half of the amount of all plastics ever produced were made during the current century and over 44 percent of this flow has been used to produce single-use packaging for commodities. This prefigures a discussion we will have in the next two chapters about how advanced capitalism grows by articulating overconsumption to overproduction.

To sum up, as the scale of throughput flows grows, new materials are progressively integrated into the fossil-industrial metabolic regime. Coal, oil, and gas, metals, cement and other mineral aggregates form the material base of the phenomenal growth of the economic process since 1800—all elements that result from geological processes and that must be extracted through mining. Harvested biomass remains an important component of the throughput. Its scale does grow, but it accounts for an ever-smaller proportion of overall flows. *Extraction* overtakes *cultiva-*

18. Roland Geyer, Jenna R. Jambeck and Kara Lavender Law, "Production, Use, and Fate of All Plastics Ever Made," *Science Advances* 3(7) (July 2017): 25–29, https://doi.org/10.1126/sciadv.1700782.

tion as the metabolic foundation of the economic process, and it is the extraction of geological stocks that sustains and nourishes the spectacular growth pattern of the fossil-industrial metabolic regime.

One could object that the exponential growth in material and energy flows we have been examining up until now in this chapter does not correspond with a deep socio-ecological transformation but is merely a reflection of another growth dynamic: population. Population growth does follow a growth pattern similar to material flows in the twentieth century, and so while in absolute terms throughput growth might seem spectacular, in per capita terms, one could argue that it would appear less dramatic. And this is true: in per capita terms, material flows multiplied by 2.6 times from 1900 to 2015, versus 12 times in absolute terms. But this is abstracting from the very real material inequalities between regions of the world we have encountered in Chapter 1. While one (small) part of the world was experiencing exponential throughput growth, other parts remained in a predominantly agrarian metabolic regime and were (and are still) experiencing fossil-industrial metabolism as mainly an exterior colonial force imposing unidirectional outflows of extracted or harvested energy and matter from peripheries to capitalist cores. Demographics do not explain the remarkable features of the fossil-industrial regime, nor its scale, nor its growth dynamic, nor the predominance of stock-building flows over purely dissipative ones.

Another more relevant metric is mass throughput per unit of world GDP. GDP estimates can give us an approximate measure of the size of the global monetary production economy in a given year. They encapsulate the unequal and uneven development of capitalist social relations the world over. Basically, the metric estimates the materiality for a given year of one unit of value (here US dollars) of produced goods and services.[19] Figure 4.7 presents the global material extraction needed to generate one US dollar of GDP for a given year.[20] As can be seen, the economic growth captured by GDP metrics shows a distinct pattern of "dematerialization" or relative decoupling between the estimate of global GDP and measures of throughput mass. In 1900, to generate $1 of GDP it was necessary to

---

19.   It includes investment good and services, consumption good and services, both consumed privately and collectively through public service.
20.   This method of examining the relationship between the economic process and the metabolic flow is taken from Krausmann et al., 2017, p. 2006.

extract and harvest 3.7kg of matter, and most (75 percent) of this was harvested biomass and much of this biomass was animal feed. In 2015, this number was down to a little more than 1.4kg of throughput for $1 of GDP. But the line labelled "the geological constant of GDP" tells a whole other story. It measures the portion of the throughput that consists of extracted matter from geological cycles: metals, non-metallic minerals and fossil energy carriers. And here, there is no sign of dematerialization or decoupling. In 1900, to generate $1 of GDP, 1kg of matter had to be extracted from geological cycles; in 2015, the amount was 1.1kg. Coupling is evident. There is some variation in time, a high point of material "inefficiency" was reached in the early 1960s, but otherwise extraction and growth are highly correlated throughout the history of the fossil-industrial metabolic regime.

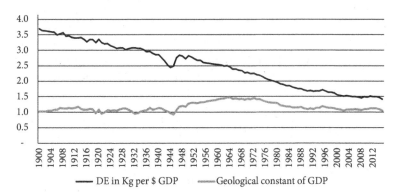

Figure 4.7   Material intensity of global economy, 1900–2015

Source: Krausmann et al., "From Resource Extraction to Outflows of Wastes and Emissions."

THE STRUCTURAL FEATURES OF FOSSIL-INDUSTRIAL METABOLISM

We now have all the empirical elements to put forward an interpretative model of fossil-industrial metabolism analog to the agrarian model we proposed in Chapter 3. The purpose of the model is to identify the structural determinants of this metabolic process and its typical dynamics, which, as presented in Table 4.1, consists of exponential growth and its particular surplus constraint.

In Chapter 1, we delineated a model of the throughput flow that was built around four successive structural moments: extraction, production, consumption and dissipation/waste. As the mass throughput flows, it goes through a series of metamorphoses that are both of social and biophysical in nature, and these moments mark these changes. This led us to furthermore insist on a conception of production and consumption as biophysical transformations,[21] the four-point model should thus be read as:

E: Point of extraction
P: Point of productive transformation
C: Point of consumptive transformation
D: Point of dissipation and waste

It was also shown that each of these moments or points is the site of a stock–flow–practice nexus, and we highlighted the varying social form of the stocks accumulated at each point, fixed capital being the predominant form at point E, P and D and durable goods, residential structures and collectively used infrastructures being the typical social form at point C. This framework allows us to analyze the nature, dynamics, constraints and specific features of fossil-industrial metabolism.

Like other metabolic regimes, the fossil-industrial regime has a biomass production and harvest–appropriation constraint. The agrarian metabolic cycle outlined in Chapter 3 is thus an important structural component of this regime, but it is not its foundation. On the contrary, biomass production and harvests are regulated by throughput flows originating in a new core metabolic cycle, the industrial–extractive complex which governs the overall throughput flow by tapping into geological stocks of matter, fossil energy carriers in particular. Productive transformation takes on an industrial form which could be defined in a myriad of ways in terms of scale, energy consumption, output form (serialized commodities) and typical relations of exploitation.

As has been documented by social ecologists (Fischer-Kowalski) and leading ecoMarxists (Burkett, Foster),[22] Marx was a precursor of the use

---

21. Breaking with the economic confusion between production–consumption of value and production, use and waste of material objects (goods) or practices (services).
22. Kohei Saito, *Karl Marx's Ecosocialism: Capital, Nature, and the Unfinished Critique of Political Economy*. New York: Monthly Review Press, 2017; John Bellamy Foster, Brett Clark and Richard York, *The Ecological Rift: Capitalism's War on the Earth*. New York: Monthly Review Press, 2010; John Bellamy Foster and Brett Clark, *The*

of metabolism as a concept to understand nature–society relations. The locus of the explicit use of the concept is in *Capital*'s study of the labor process in Chapter 7, or more specifically an analysis of the production process as the unity of the labor process and the valorization process. Marx begins by examining the production of use-values as a transhistorical and universal feature of social life, before examining its mediation in capitalist production by the imperative of surplus-value production and introducing the historically specific social relations that subsume the labor process in this mode of production.[23] The labor process brings together, in a dialectical form, three "elementary factors": 1. personal activity or work; 2. the subject of that work; and 3. the instruments of labor "a thing, or a complex of things, which the laborer interposes between himself and the subject of his labor, and which serves as the conductor of his activity." This dialectical structure of production found in *Capital* had been an object of study by Marx since the economic manuscripts of 1844 and is schematically illustrated in Figure 4.8. It is built around three dialectical elements: S–M–O, labor as a subject–object relation mediated by a third tier. In the labor process, this mediating tier is itself a three-tier structure: "the instruments of labor" brings together nature, tools and materials, tools and materials being the objective factors drawn from nature and consumed in the labor process by the working subject with the finality of producing a given use-value. And as argued by Marx in the 1844 manuscripts, it is through this labor process that nature itself is socialized as a historical world.[24]

For Marx, whether the laborer engages freely in this process in and for himself like the proverbial Cincinnatus tilling his field or if it is done under conditions of exploitation through wage labor or slavery does not change the form of this metabolic process.

Robbery of Nature: Capitalism and the Ecological Rift. New York: Monthly Review Press, 2020; Paul Burkett, *Marx and Nature: A Red Green Perspective*. Chicago, IL: Haymarket Books, 2014; and Paul Burkett and John Bellamy Foster, *Marx and the Earth: An Anti-Critique*. Chicago, IL: Haymarket Books, 2019.

23. We have found this method of inquiry and of exposition particularly useful for the organization of our analysis in this book.

24. On this, see Franck Fischbach, *Sans Objet: Capitalisme, subjectivité, aliénation*. Paris: Vrin, 2009. I have explored this in Éric Pineault, "Capital, valeur et réversibilité: recherche sur les fondements de l'approche marxienne du capital financier," *Marx Philosophe*, ed. Olivier Clain (Quebec: Nota Bene, 2009), on which much of this section is based.

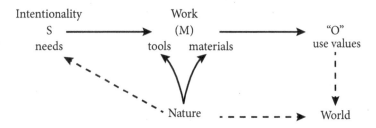

Figure 4.8 The labor process as metabolism
Source: Author.

Industry is based on the subversion and inversion of this form through the development of what Marx has called machinery and what we call the machine process. In the machine process, the starting point of production is not the intentionality and bodily force of the laborer, it is the machine itself and the prime mover which animates its artificial body. The laborer is a component of this self-acting and automated process of production.[25] And as the machine process subsumes other forms of production, it will find in the steam engine the ideal prime mover and material foundation for its development. But, as Marx remarks, for the steam engine to become the general source of work would require that it be produced by machines on a mass scale. And though Marx does not give this aspect much analytical importance, the development of machines capable of producing other machines, steam engines in particular, implies access to mass flows of the materials used in their construction, in this case iron and steel, as well as coal, oil and gas, the geological stocks on which the fossil-industrial metabolic regime is founded. Finally, this system also implies and is driven by the need to deploy evermore power per unit of work, and, in a recursive manner, the more powerful the machines, the more material transformations can be intense, the more the volume of matter that can be extracted, put into circulation, productively transformed, consumed, accumulated and dissipated.[26]

25. "Every kind of capitalist production, in so far as it is not only a labor-process, but also a process of creating surplus-value, has this in common, that it is not the workman that employs the instruments of labor, but the instruments of labor that employ the workman. But it is only in the factory system that this inversion for the first time acquires technical and palpable reality." Marx, *Captial*, Chapter 15, section 4.
26.   For example, the regular consumption of craft beer in small disposable aluminum cans is something completely unfathomable in a society without advanced machinery and access to cheap sources of bauxite through asymmetric flows of matter.

To put this into perspective, Table 4.2 compares the maximum power provided by some typical prime movers existing when the fossil-industrial metabolic regime emerged and adds two industrial mining machines typically used today to extract coal, metal ores, phosphates, potash, limestone and other critical minerals as well as tar sands. To expend the same amount of power as one of these machines in an agrarian regime would imply collecting and condensing the work of 80,000 human beings or 8,000 work animals. Even the relatively primitive Watt and Boulton steam engine condensed the power of 800 laborers or 80 work animals. The much more powerful Corliss type engines that not only drove spinning machines, but also worked steel, wrought iron and powered steamboats in the mid-nineteenth century condensed the power of 5,000 to 15,000 laborers.

Table 4.2 Power and the socio-metabolic transition

Prime mover	Power measured in horsepower
Human using a tool	0.05hp
Work animal (horse, ox, donkey)	0.5hp
Watermill (circa 1750)	3hp
Windmill (circa 1750)	8hp
Newcomen steam engine (circa 1712)	5hp
Watt's steam engine (circa 1776)	40hp
Corliss type steam engine (circa 1870)	100–300hp
Caterpillar 797F dump truck*	4,000hp
O&K RH400 Hydraulic Shovel** (both used in mining circa 2020)	4,500hp

Source: Astrid Kander, Paolo Malanima and Paul Warde, *Power to the People: Energy in Europe Over the Last Five Centuries*. Princeton, NJ: Princeton University Press, 2013.
Note:
*www.cat.com/en_US/products/new/equipment/off-highway-trucks/mining-trucks/18093014.html
** https://machine.market/specification-20915

As remarked by Marx, the individual nineteenth-century capitalists who invested and then put these machines to work had access to power at a scale unheard of in human history. It is these machines that mediated the extractive process of fossil industrial society, the scope and scale of what could be extracted and transformed by industrial processes grew as exponentially as the development of the capacity to do work of these industrial machines. It is in this very precise sense that Wrigley's rule has explanatory relevance. A fossil-based industrial economy has lowering marginal costs as output grows because of the social metabolic relations that arise around machinery. This machine capacity opened up not only new extractive frontiers that were previously inaccessible to society, but also drove the capacity to industrially transform new forms of matter. It paved the way to today's "omnivorous" metabolism where almost all elements of the periodic table are systematically extracted, transformed and dissipated, having become essential to the social metabolism of advanced capitalist societies.[27]

From a socio-metabolic perspective, a machine is a stock, a manufactured artifact, and as such the laws and principles that govern their material existence and relations to the throughput apply to machines. But machines have their own particular relationship to the throughput flow, their mode of existence is oriented toward the transformation of matter and the consumption of energy. They exist to command flows, and they do so through the mobilization and absorption of labor power. Even a computing machine such as a smart phone cannot compute immaterially; it depends on the flow of electrons in a processor to accomplish its dematerialized tasks. And thus, most smart phones existing in the world today command flows of coal to exist. A machine then can be conceptualized as a nexus of relations between the artifact, the material and energy flows that animate its existence and which it consumes and the social practices it mobilizes and reproduces. Getting back to the relationship between stocks and flows particular to machines, because of their power, machines depend on mass flows on an incommensurable scale compared to the flows commanded by the artifacts and stocks of agrarian societies. In terms of composition, a significant proportion of these flows tend to be of materials of geological origin which are readily available because of the "Bunker effects" presented at the beginning of this chapter.

Figure 4.9 presents the overall metabolic structure of fossil-industrial societies.

---

27. See Aaron Greenfield and T.E. Graedel, "The Omnivorous Diet of Modern Technology," *Resources, Conservation and Recycling* 74 (2013): 1–7, https://doi. org/10.1016/j.resconrec.2013.02.010.

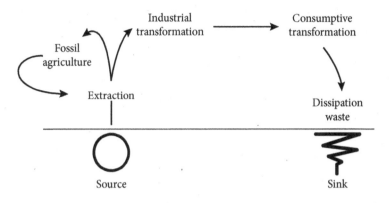

Figure 4.9 Structure of fossil industrial metabolism
Source: Author.

The Point of Extraction

There are two functionally distinct points of extraction in this model. A first is the agrarian metabolic cycle which mobilizes nature's work in the form of ecological productivity to extract a produced biological surplus through harvests. This matter enters into the metabolism of industrial society as biomass fed into the sphere of industrial productive transformation dominated by the machine process. This could be felled trees absorbed by a pulp and paper mill, living animals entering a mega-slaughterhouse, or palm fruits entering a biorefinery. But this outflow of biomass from the agrarian cycle is mirrored by an inflow of industrial products—in particular dissipative matter such as fertilizers and pesticides—that regulate the biological productivity of agriculture. In energetic terms, the agrarian cycle does not produce a surplus, it is a sink; fossil-industrial societies use the geological surplus of energy contained in fossil fuels to subsidize the biological productivity of agro-ecosystems. From the perspective of energy analysis, modern agriculture (and aquaculture as well as some forms of tree farming such as Brazilian eucalyptus plantations) is a rather inefficient energy conversion system.[28] That said, this inflow of energy and matter is what replaces

---

28. For an example based on Quebec, but typical of most fossil-based agro-systems, see Lluis Parcerisas and Jérôme Dupras, "From Mixed Farming to Intensive Agriculture: Energy Profiles of Agriculture in Quebec, Canada, 1871–2011," *Regional*

labor in the agro-ecological cycle, freeing up people from the constraint of agricultural work and sustaining the development of urban lifestyles and the urbanization of society where a mere 5 percent of the population can generate the biomass for the other 95 percent in an inversed ratio to agrarian societies.[29] This inversion has its ecological corollary in the biogeochemical cycles of nitrogen and phosphorous that are today subsumed by anthropic flows of fertilizers.

The second tier of material extraction is the extractive sector per se based on mining of geological stocks of matter: metals, non-metallic minerals such as limestone, phosphates, potash or uranium and fossil fuels (coal, oil and gas) as well as more recently trace metals and substances tied to the development of electronics. Whereas the first tier involves interacting with ecosystems—in particular sinking labor in artificialized agro-ecosystems, extraction implies considering ecosystems as "mort terrain" to use an expression from the mining industry, literally "dead land." Space acquires a third dimension as extraction delves below the surface in a mode of occupation that has been characterized as "punctiform" instead of "areal." Of course, this distinction is for subsurface mines and does not apply to surface mining or extreme forms of subsurface extraction such as fracking which can take a very "areal form." As we observed at the beginning of this chapter, a more relevant distinction is between these pre-existing stocks of useful matter which take on a "surplus form" in an immediate fashion and the agro-ecological constraint of growing a stock of useful matter by participating in net primary production.

Because of investment in the scaling up of the extractive capacity of mineral stocks in all forms, there is a tendency of overabundance of extractive flows of geological matter. The result is a push effect: the throughput flow between the point productive transformation and the point extraction is not necessarily governed by the functional needs of the former, it is often governed by the imperative of extraction of the latter,

Environmental Change 18(4) (2018): 1047–1057, https://doi.org/10.1007/s10113-018-1305-y.

29. How this could be sustained in a post-fossil metabolic regime remains a *"non-dit"* in most transition debates. For a sobering discussion of the implications, see Alevgul H. Sorman and Mario Giampietro, "The Energetic Metabolism of Societies and the Degrowth Paradigm: Analyzing Biophysical Constraints and Realities," *Journal of Cleaner Production* 38 (2013): 80–93, https://doi.org/10.1016/j.jclepro.2011.11.059.

especially when this extractive process is mediated by capitalist social property relations. In that specific case, the extractive flow is governed by a valorization imperative which we will study in the next chapters.

The Point of Productive Transformation

We have already encountered the logic and dynamics of the point of productive transformation through our prior discussion of the machine process. An important aspect we outlined is the self-reinforcing loop between extraction and industrial production not only through the production of specialized extractive machines but also through the constant adaptation at the point of production to the scale and nature of the mass flows of extracted matter. The relatively long lifespans of the industrial machines that form the heart of the point of productive transformation of the throughput tend to lock in and reinforce existing patterns of extraction. As argued by Malm, the capacity of industrial machinery to absorb and organize labor power is determined by the quantum of fossil fuels burnt to animate prime movers. But other material flows of geological origin are also critical as the race for rare earths exemplifies. The capacity to extract ever-greater amounts of massified and serialized raw matter sustains the possibility for the industrial production of a commodified throughput with the same characteristics.

The Point of Consumptive Transformation

The machine process of industrial transformation spews a continuous mass flow of serialized use-values and constructs massive built structures such as residences and transport infrastructure. The social relation to this metabolic flow is organized by the stock-flow-practice nexus at the point of consumption. At this point, reproductive social activity is articulated and mediated to the throughput as well as accumulated artifacts. One way of reading the epochal growth process known as the Great Acceleration is to examine how it is driven by the accumulation of artifacts that have a tendency to subsume the reproductive sphere through the development of mass consumption as a form of social activity. And how a defining feature of the artifacts that mediate this subsumption process is their existence as machines analogous to those in the productive sphere, generalizing fossil-fuel-based energy demand—in particular in the form of automobile use and the urban form that it favors. The other salient feature is the construction of a built urban environment of concrete structures that tendentially incorporate evermore animated functions and processes with high energy and material requirements, structures which, when compared to wood, brick and stone buildings and infrastructures are surprisingly short lived. This results in high churn rate for concrete-based built stocks.

The Point of Dissipation and Waste

Mass extraction and mass production imply evidently mass waste flows. This is compounded by the fact that the specific form taken by mass production in advanced capitalism entails a built-in limit to use as well as imperatives to waste that are locked into the material form and symbolic dimension of reproductive and consumptive artifacts. All societies biophysically regulate and symbolically mark their waste flows. What characterizes the regulation in this regime is the accumulation of functionally distinct artifacts in the form of infrastructure and machinery to mediate the metabolic frontier with sinks. And, as elsewhere, at the point of dissipation stocks command flows. The development of the capacity to regulate mass dissipative flows becomes a driver of throughput growth in its own right. The chimney, the sewer and dump are not new forms of waste flow and sink management, but they are brought up to a scale that is incommensurable to what prior agrarian societies had developed. This scaling up is an extensive process and materializes as the growth of the size of these mediating structures (taller chimneys, more extensive sewage collection systems, mega-landfills), their number and density. But scaling up dissipative flows is also done through intensive forms of accumulation, by accruing the amount of biophysical work sunk into evermore complex dissipative structures. An interesting example is the technical evolution of the automobile tailpipe and exhaust systems throughout the last century, as ever-more sophisticated exhaust systems have permitted the growth and concentration in urban environments of an ever-greater amount of internal combustion engines. An extreme example is contemporary carbon capture, use and sequestration systems where injected CO_2 is used to squeeze more hydrocarbons out of oil and gas wells.

STRUCTURAL LIMITS OF FOSSIL-INDUSTRIAL
METABOLISM AS WHOLE

Though fossil-industrial metabolism overcomes the constraints faced by the agrarian metabolic regime, it comes up against constraints of its own. Two obvious constraints that have been the focus of much reflection on the structural limits to growth of this regime are source depletion and sink saturation. Depletion of geological stocks has haunted this regime since its emergence (see work by Jevons on the coal question in late 1800s)[30] and today, because of the so-called "omnivorous" nature of the throughput, this constraint has been intensified. More interesting though is the way society has reacted to these constraints by investing in the expansion of the capacity to extract and sink which has displaced the frontier of these limits without actually overcoming them. Two other constraints are the biophysical limits in efficiency of the machine process that arises between extraction and productive transformation, or limits to "work" and most importantly the constraint that emerges between production and consumption which takes the form of an absorption constraint. The former is precisely the material and practical context that nourished the rise and development of the physics of thermodynamics and engineering. The second became a core concern in the science of economics as the problem of effective demand. Are the social practices that congeal around the reproductive sphere capable of absorbing the mass throughput that comes out of the point of production? The analysis of these limits and constraints, as well as those that arise in the subsumed sphere of biomass production, implies that we shift our argument from metabolism in the abstract, to the capitalist form that presided over the development of this metabolic regime.

THE TRAJECTORY OF GROWTH OF
FOSSIL-INDUSTRIAL METABOLISM

We have discussed the fossil-industrial metabolic regime in the singular as if it was a single undifferentiated type. This abstract ideal typical

---

30. Brett Clark and John Bellamy Foster, "William Stanley Jevons and the Coal Question: An Introduction to Jevons's 'Of the Economy of Fuel,'" *Organization & Environment* 14(1) (2001): 93–98, https://doi.org/10.1177/1086026601141005.

analysis must not hide the very wide discrepancy and variation of metabolic rates and profiles between societies both in time and space. Energy and material consumption and accumulation rates vary and are highly unequal between societies, something that was shown in Chapter 1, and inside societies between social groups. Furthermore, these differences are neither accidental nor natural; they are the product of relations of differential appropriation, of exploitation and of externalization that have a structural character between hegemonic cores of accumulation and peripheries[31] as well as between classes, gender and races.[32]

A significant part of humanity lives today in societies which overall are still determined by the logic and dynamics of the agrarian metabolic regime. Subsistence farming and gardening remain a dominant mode of living in many regions of the world. In these communities, fossil fuels, industrial artifacts and fossil-fueled power artifacts as well as the built environment organized around their use do exist, but the vast majority of individuals are constrained by the imperative to produce a biophysical surplus through agriculture (subsidized by fossil fuels) and their livelihoods depend on local and regional circuits of distribution even though marginally they tap into global commodity chains as producers or consumers. This is actually a historical characteristic of the fossil-industrial metabolic regime. It has coexisted through time with the agrarian regime in a relation that has changed and evolved but never disappeared. The notion of metabolic transition should be understood as an unequal, partial and articulated process. The exponential growth process of the fossil-industrial regime implied articulations and material interdependencies with agrarian regions and societies that pushed their development in certain directions.

Industrial Britain relied on the slave plantation system for its sugar and for the cotton that was transformed in Manchester. It relied on wheat from Russia and Canada, timber from North American and Scandinavian forests, all of which were harvested and hauled by human and animal muscles, then shipped and transported with wind and waterpower. Fossil fuels, so important to the growth process of nineteenth-century Great

---

31. Ulrich Brand and Markus Wissen, *Imperial Mode of Living: Everyday Life and the Ecological Crisis of Capitalism*, trans. Zachary King. London: Verso, 2021.
32. For an analysis of these dynamics, see Gargi Bhattacharyya, *Rethinking Racial Capitalism: Questions of Reproduction and Survival*. London: Rowman & Littlefield, 2018.

Britain, were marginal in Canada throughout the same century: in 1870, coal provided 7 percent of the country's energy needs whereas fuelwood provided 82 percent (the ratio at this time in the UK is 95 percent for coal and 0 percent for wood) yet, during this period, Canada was a major exporter of wood and wheat to the United Kingdom.[33] And both material expansions were made possible by the genocidal dispossession of primarily hunting-gathering native peoples from their traditional lands and territories by white settler agriculturalists. As we have seen, this articulation is actually a structural aspect of the fossil-industrial regime's mode of integrating and articulating its geological foundation to its agro-ecological cycle. The historical particularity here being that this articulation brings together two different societies—though united in a relation of colonial dependence.

This leads us to another important distinction: the development of the fossil-industrial regime in the capitalist core was not a linear and merely quantitative process; it was itself uneven and variegated in terms of material composition and typical extractive, productive, consumptive and dissipative social relations. At a very abstract and general level, we can distinguish two historical phases that mark the trajectory of growth of the fossil-industrial regime: a first phase, where the regime is formed around the extraction and transformation of coal, iron and steel; and a second phase, where oil, gas and cement become key "regime forming" elements of the throughput in addition to coal, iron and steel. The second phase corresponds with the period social ecologists and environmental historians have named the Great Acceleration; the first covers the classical Industrial Revolution.

The trajectory of growth of this regime, and in fact its institutional and material features, were fashioned by capitalist social relations. The agrarian regime saw capitalist social relations emerge in its midst and grow into a recognizable economy and society in England and spread as its commercial empire changed into an empire of capital,[34] but its growth and development remained constrained by the structural features

33. Data published by Joint Center for History and Economics, Harvard University and University of Cambridge. Energy History. https://sites.fas.harvard.edu/~histecon/energyhistory/energydata_beta.html.
34. Ellen Meiksins Wood, *Empire of Capital*. London: Verso, 2005.

of the agrarian regime we highlighted in Chapter 3.[35] The fossil-industrial metabolic regime is a creature of capitalist development and accumulation. This leads us to a discussion of capital as a mediation of social metabolism.

---

35. Many of these constraints were identified and studied by classical political economists Smith, Ricardo and Malthus. On this, see E.A. Wrigley's *Energy and the English Industrial Revolution* (Cambridge: Cambridge University Press, 2010) and his concept of England as an "advanced organic economy" during the period leading up to the Industrial Revolution from 1600 to 1800. This concept can also be applied to the Netherlands during the same period.

5

On Capitalist Metabolism

the measure of advancement of "advanced capitalism" has become the efficacy with which waste can be generated and dissipated on a monumental scale.

István Mészáros, *Beyond Capital*[1]

Matter will not flow by itself through social structures on an entropic journey toward dissipation, nor will it accumulate and congeal into artifacts of steel, plastic or cement on its own. Matter works through its potentialities, but matter either as mass flows or as accumulated artifacts, does not have agency.[2] Hydrocarbons, to take a core element of social metabolism today for both social and ecological reasons, represent a radically slowed down component of the carbon cycle, flowing at a speed only perceptible from the vantage point of geological time.[3] For hydrocarbons to provoke climate change, this cycle must be accelerated and forced, more carbon must leave the Earth's crust than is geologically sequestered in bogs, swamps and other anaerobic marine environments. The unbalanced acceleration of this flow is what "causes" climate change, yet one cannot attribute global warming to coal, oil or gas. The same could be said of the phosphorous and nitrogen cycles that are also deeply impacted by social metabolism and have disrupted marine and freshwater ecosystems. Nor, finally, does matter flow or accumulate in order to service human needs in the abstract. Matter is extracted, transformed, used and dissipated in a nexus of capitalist social relations that drive the throughput process.

---

1. István Mészáros, *Beyond Capital: Toward a Theory of Transition*. New York: Monthly Review Press, 1995, 547.
2. Alf Hornborg, *Nature, Society and Justice in the Anthropocene: Unraveling the Money-Energy-Technology Complex*. Cambridge: Cambridge University Press, 2019.
3. Jeremy Davies, *The Birth of the Anthropocene*. Oakland, CA: University of California Press, 2018.

As we have seen in Chapter 4, a significant proportion of the flow of matter in the last 200 years has been governed by the machine process and this process is, itself, an expression of capitalist social relations of production. The machine process, a "'stock-flow and practice nexus'" is the effective—material—mediation of the vast throughput flows that have resulted in an accumulation of stocks of titanesque scale, matching in mass existing biomass. The question then is what drives the machine process, the throughput flow and the vast accumulation of stocks in the fossil-industrial metabolic regime.

MARX ON ACCUMULATION AND THE CAPITALIST GROWTH IMPERATIVE

That capitalist economies are compelled to grow is usually attributed to the imperative of accumulation, in reference to Marx's *Capital* this can be illustrated by the simple but powerful M–C–M' formula. Money (M) becomes capital (M') as a result of a valorization process, where surplus value has been drawn out of productive activity based on the exploitation wage labor (C). If this surplus value is validated in the ensuing realization process, the surplus value carrying commodities are sold "at value" and not at cost, the capitalist comes out with a greater amount of money than when he entered the sphere of production. On the other side, the laborer comes out as he entered, with just enough monetary income to cover his subsistence costs so that he or she can come and work the next day. With each cycle of production, the capitalist accumulates ever-more money to be transformed as capital through valorization and realization processes that imply expanding production, an accumulation spiral drives economic growth.

For Marx, capitalism is a *monetary production economy*, the finality of the economic process that drives the metabolic process is the accumulation of capital which ultimately takes on a money form. Money is here defined as an entitlement to future social wealth—the valued output—in the abstract, freed from any substantive determinations.[4] Future social

---

4. This definition of money, though compatible with Marxian understanding of capitalist accumulation is drawn from Simmel rather than Marx. Marx remained imprisoned in a commodity theory of money, even though at times it seems his approach was on the verge of surpassing this classical understanding of money—in particular in the study of the value-form in Chapter 1, section 3 of *Capital*. Simmel

ON CAPITAL METABOLISM

wealth at one remove is future social labor and the biophysical flows out of which labor will carve the valued output. Abstract future social wealth is thus future social labor abstracted and as yet undetermined. Furthermore, in a capitalist context, social labor exists as labor separated from its means of production, which from the standpoint of social ecology exists as a stock and flow nexus. So, we can add that the power to command "future social wealth" is the power to command future flows and the building up and use of future stocks in the abstract.

Separated as much in the future as in the present from the means of production, accumulation reproduces a producer unable to autonomously activate on his or her own terms his or her productive or creative powers not only for expressive purposes but also for subsistence purposes. Having no significant access to tools, materials, space, be it land or buildings, often to markets, his or her productive and creative powers can only by activated through the sale of labor power as a commodity to a capitalist who does have access to these means of production and distribution of social wealth. Wage dependent labor is the ideal-typical form that social labor takes in a capital accumulating economy. It is in the wage labor and capital relation that the modern economic separation between production and consumption takes form as well as its mediation by monetized relations.[5]

---

offers a much more productive starting point for a theory of money as an institutional mediation of social practice and relations. Éric Pineault, "Réification et massification du capital financier: une contribution à la théorie critique de la financiarisation à partir de l'analyse de la titrisation," *Cahiers de Recherche Sociologique* 55 (2013): 117–154, https://doi.org/10.7202/1027684ar.

5.   The monetary integration of capitalist economies also implies closure and totality of circulation. In a monetary economy, incomes are the result of expenditures, and expenditures are derived from incomes. This means that, in contradistinction to the biophysical throughput, monetary flows are circular in nature and the units have the attribute of reversibility—if we ignore inflation. Growth is possible because in capitalist economies there are forms of autonomous expenditures which flow out of credit relations based on the social production of "endogenous" bank money. Two classes of agents in capitalism have historically monopolized autonomous expenditures: capitalists and the state. All other agents must receive monetary income in some form or another before they can spend. In regulation theory, this is known as the monetary constraint of capitalist economies. This also means that monetary expenditures cannot—ontologically—compensate in any way for material or biophysical costs, losses or destruction. Monetary expenditure can only flow toward a being that can accumulate and spend the acquired income by buying something or paying a debt. For a general Marxist discussion of the implications of considering capitalism as a

121

In fine, accumulation in a capitalist form is the production of entitlements on future productive social activity as wage labor and on material flows as throughput. It was Rosa Luxemburg who forcefully argued that the accumulation of these entitlements implies the imperative to expand social activity as abstract wage labor in the future. Because labor is necessarily mediated by the material nexus of stocks and flows, this implies expanded extraction, transformation and dissipation of the mass throughput, as much as it implies expanding the sphere of commodified and value-bearing output of goods and services. This growth imperative of capitalism is not an accidental, marginal feature of this form of the economic process; it is its very essence as a monetary production economy based on accumulation. Accumulation of capital may seem to be directionless, aimless, which it is to some degree, and this stems from the fact that capital is accumulated in a money form, and so it also seems infinite and boundless. But defined in the Marxian tradition as expanded reproduction, the process does have an aim, a direction, a purpose, that being the reproduction on an ever-larger scale of the social relations that permit the transformation of money into capital; or put another way, the expansion of the accumulation process itself and the social and ecological relations it entails, what we have studied as fossil-industrial metabolism.

Malm, in *Fossil Capital*, has shown how this accumulation process in the capitalist core (England, then USA and then Western Europe) came to depend on fossil fuels as a strategic input in the production process. [6] He proposed to amend the Marxian formula of accumulation to include the combustion of fossil fuels (here FF) as a necessary material mediation of the valorization process:

$$M - C ..FF+P \ C'-M' + CO_2$$

monetary production economy, see Costas Lapavitsas, *Social Foundations of Markets, Money, and Credit*. London: Routledge, 2003, 49; and Riccardo Bellofiore, "Augusto Graziani and the Marx–Schumpeter–Keynes 'Cycle of Money Capital': A Personal Look at the Early Italian Circuitism from an Insider," *Review of Political Ecomony* 31(4) (2019): 528–558, https://doi.org/10.1080/09538259.2020.1748306. On the notion of monetary constraint, see Jean Cartelier, "Marx's Value, Exchange, and Surplus Value Theory: A Suggested Interpretation," The Jerome Levy Economics Institute Bard College, Working Paper No. 26, 1989, www.levyinstitute.org/publications/marxs-value-exchange-and-surplus-value-theory.
6.   Andreas Malm, *Fossil Capital: The Rise of Steam Power and the Roots of Global Warming*. London: Verso, 2016.

The original capitalist intention being the role coal-fired steam engines played in the real subsumption of labor through the development of the machine process in the textile industry. Fossil fuels also powered flexibly the productive process in ways that did not imply cooperation among capitalists as did a machine process based on water as a prime mover. Coal-fired steam engines were thus compatible with the social property relations and market relations typical of an early competitive phase of capitalist development.

Without this fossil input, argues Malm, the output growth rates that characterized Western societies since the nineteenth century would not have been possible.[7] If the development of fossil-fuel-based production technologies was neither a historical nor a natural necessity, once capitalist development had integrated fossil fuels into its social relations of production as a way to organize the labor process as a machine process, they would come to define the overall trajectory of capitalist accumulation. Our analysis of the fossil-industrial metabolic regime entails a more complex integration between biophysical flows and the valorization process, with more diverse materialities involved. We summarized this as E + M flows tied to the labor and machine process (K + L).

In the Marxian tradition, this accumulation of capital unfolds in two ideal-typical forms: extensive and intensive.[8] Extensive accumulation represents a quantitative expansion of the economic process that results in more use-values produced, which takes the form of more commodified means of production (constant capital) and more commodified means of subsistence (variable capital) supporting a growing commodified labor force, and thus a growing population of laborers, and an expanding material throughput. From a social ecological perspective, this means the expanded reproduction of existing relations between labor, artifacts and the throughput (fixed coefficients between these factors from an economic point of view), and once value has been realized, expanded reproduction of existing use patterns and consumptive practices, including norms of waste and dissipation in the reproductive sphere. The biophysical and ecological dimensions of extensive accumulation take the

---

7. Malm, *Fossil Capital*.
8. These two concepts are taken from the regulation school approach of political economy and here are given a wider and more critical significance. But contra the regulation approach, I do not see these forms as mutually exclusive, in any given accumulation regime they are intertwined.

form of the growth of extractive and agro-industrial production without any significant change in their metabolic efficiency nor any change in the composition of the throughput or in any new pattern of material stock formation. Colloquially, one could summarize this pattern as "more of the same." Yet this expansion does have specific biophysical characteristics, the most important being the "Bunker effects" studied in Chapter 4 and tied to the massification of the throughput flow.

Expanding demand for raw materials and energy has a recursive effect on the scale of extraction and thus on the circulation of extracted matter. Larger means of circulation cheapens the per unit cost of the extracted throughput, which further sustains its penetration in the metabolic profile of the economic process, widening and locking in its use without implying any enhanced productivity in the extractive process per se. Given the paradox of abundance that determines the extractive flow of most of the core geological sources of matter of fossil-industrial metabolism, this invisiblizes any eventual peak supply problems.[9] Finally, as also argued by Rosa Luxemburg, extensive accumulation materializes spatially as the geographical expansion, extension and reach of capitalist social relations of production and consummation in colonial, neocolonial and imperial forms. Far from equalizing, homogenizing and universalizing the conditions of exploitation and realization that prevails in the advanced capitalist core, this expansion frontier espouses and enhances differences and produces heterogeneities along ethnic, racialized and gendered lines.[10] The same spatial and global heterogeneities appear in the ecological conditions of extraction, production and waste, as capital espouses "the paths of least resistance."[11]

Intensive accumulation refers to the qualitative change of social and metabolic relations through the ability of capitalism to "grow on itself" by constantly destroying given extraction and production relations through productivity-enhancing investments, which in Marxian terms

9.   It is also a key component of the machine fetishism explored by Hornborg; see Alf Hornborg, *The Magic of Technology: The Machine as a Transformation of Slavery.* Abingdon: Routledge, 2022.
10.   Gargi Bhattacharyya, *Rethinking Racial Capitalism: Questions of Reproduction and Survival.* London: Rowman and Littlefield, 2018.
11.   István Mészáros, *Beyond Capital: Towards a Theory of Transition.* New York: Monthly Review Press, 2010. See also Jason W. Moore, *Capitalism in the Web of Life: Ecology and the Accumulation of Capital.* New York: Verso, 2015.

takes the form of a rising ratio of constant capital to variable capital—or, in more common terms—more machines and better tools per given unit of labor. This translates into more throughput per unit of expended labor unless there is a change in the material content of the throughput. It can imply more efficient use of the material throughput, by the development of matter and energy-saving innovations, though, because of the Bunker effect on circulation discussed earlier, the inducements to do so are tempered in industrial capitalism. And as Jevons observed in the nineteenth century, material efficiency often leads, through rebound effects, to a higher energy and material throughput.[12] Qualitative change in the metabolic profile because of intensive accumulation has followed a different path during the last century and a half. It has taken the form of a transition from a limited ensemble of elements extracted and transformed into relatively simple forms—iron into steel, limestone into cement, oil into fuel and eventually into plastics, natural gas into ammonium-based fertilizers in the first half of the twentieth century to the omnivorous flow of molecularly complex and composite materials used today. Intensive accumulation has also implied higher energy consumption per unit of labor expended, as well as machinery able to expend and put to work more of these intense flows of energy, and an overall expansion of the mediation of social activity by machine and the embedding of machines in infrastructure and in the built environment.

Figure 5.1 traces this growth of energy expended per unit of labor hour worked in the USA during the twentieth century as an example of this dynamic.

Figure 5.2, which is drawn from the same sources, provides a more refined view of this energetic mediation by tracing the contribution of the different physical forms of work to the energetic metabolism of the United States and comparing this again to the mass of labor time expended per year over the twentieth century. Muscle work does grow from 60 to 80pj per hour, but this is small when compared to the growth of mechanical and electric work which reached 130pj per labor hour in the 1970s. Their growth is directly tied to the energy needs of animated artifacts in the

---

12. Brett Clark and John Bellamy Foster, "William Stanley Jevons and the Coal Question: An Introduction to Jevons's 'Of the Economy of Fuel,'" *Organization & Environment* 14(1) (2001): 93–98, https://doi.org/10.1177/1086026601141005.

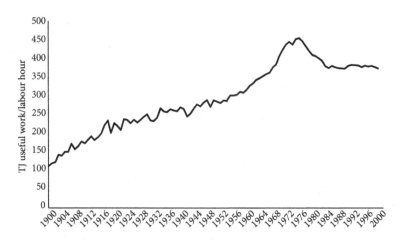

Figure 5.1   Energizing the labor hour: US experience, 1900–2000

Source: Benjamin Warr, Robert Ayres, Nina Eisenmenger, Fridolin Krausmann and Heinz Schandl, "Energy Use and Economic Development: A Comparative Analysis of Useful Work Supply in Austria, Japan, the United Kingdom and the US during 100years of Economic Growth," *Ecological Economics* 69(10) (2010): 1904–1917. https://doi.org/10.1016/j.ecolecon.2010.03.021.

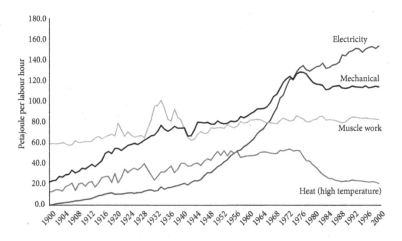

Figure 5.2   Useful work per labor hour, 1900–2000

Source: Warr et al., "Energy Use and Economic Development."

sphere of production and consumption resulting from an intensive accumulation pattern.

So, from a strictly biophysical perspective, the material productivity of intensive accumulation often results in more entropy, not less. A further outcome of intensive accumulation is the destruction of given consumption relations and the introduction of new use-values, which revolutionizes the subsistence patterns of laborers and the reproductive work of women, as well as changing social activity in general, and producing new social norms of dissipation and waste.

Though we have distinguished, for strictly analytical purposes, extensive and intensive forms of accumulation, in the real process of capital accumulation they are intertwined forces. In standard economic language, these two forms of accumulation are understood as two complementary forms of investment: capital widening (extensive) and capital deepening (intensive). Investment in a capitalist monetary production economy is the social power to initiate and direct the accumulation process for private purpose, knowing that the ultimate outcome is the expanded reproduction of the capitalist form of the economic and metabolic process. Investment is thus a very powerful form of socio-ecological power in the sense that he who invests in extensive or intensive forms constructs and determines the economic and metabolic future of society, produces determined forms of social production as labor, produces future forms of consumption, directs the accumulation of matter and finally controls how fixed capital will accumulate in specific artifact forms at all points of the metabolic flow, from extraction to dissipation. Capitalist investment is historical force, a socio-ecological form of historicity. But more importantly, every act of investment constructs, and determines concretely, the effective relation between economic growth and material growth as throughput, capital's social ecology. The economic process in capitalism emerges in the field between these two dimensions. This is illustrated in Figure 5.3 as a valorization process that implies both the production of value through the exploitation of productive labor and the production of the entropic flow through biophysical work, a plane of materiality that Marx captured through his concept of "use-value."[13] An important

---

13. As we saw in Chapter 1, from the standpoint of metabolic analysis, use-value captures just one of the metamorphoses of matter as it flows from one entropic transformation to another.

feature of this mode of representing the articulation of value and entropic transformation is that they are not reducible to one another. The process of capitalist valorization necessarily involves entropic dissipation; there can be no production of capitalist value without production entropy, but entropy is not value. Yes, the slope of the line that represents the results of the valorization process could shift upwards or downwards and this would reflect a change in the material efficiency of capitalist extraction and production. But as illustrated, there are zones of impossibility in Figure 5.3 (in light gray): at the bottom, biophysical work not mediated by productive labor is not capitalist valorization, and at the top, exploitation of productive labor without an entropic flow goes against basic biophysical laws. Yet paradoxically, both correspond to capitalist utopias (and each has its socialist fan club), the first of an entirely automated economic process and the second of an entirely dematerialized process of valorization.

Accumulation implies more than valorization, it is necessarily followed by a process of realization of value as consumption and then, because use-values are material, a waste process. The first two moments of

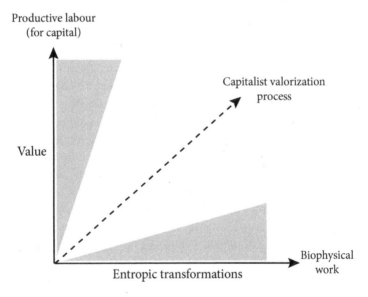

Figure 5.3 Capital and Entropy
Source: Author.

expanded reproduction are extensively discussed by Marx in *Capital* and have their correspondence in his formula of accumulation, the latter moment, corresponds to the point where the material throughput enters the lower zone of impossibility in Figure 5.3, matter works and flows but is unmediated by *productive* labor. Yet this metamorphosis of the material throughput does not happen on its own; as argued at the beginning of this chapter, it is mediated by social practices (and also stocks, more on this later). In Marx's categories these practices correspond to *socially necessary but unproductive labor* from the standpoint of capital.[14]

Figure 5.4 illustrates, in a complete fashion, the metabolic structure of the accumulation of capital by tracing how the mass throughput flow is mediated by the valorization and realization imperatives of a capitalist monetary production economy before losing all value in the capitalist waste process as it flows toward dissipation. It articulates these imperatives to the four moments of the metabolic process outlined in previous chapters: as value is extracted through the exploitation of productive labor and realized in circulation, matter and energy are entropically extracted (E), productively and consumptively transformed (P and C) and then dissipated (D) as waste, which corresponds to unproductive but socially necessary practices and labor. These are the specifically capitalist relations that drive and shape the throughput flow in a basic Marxian framework. From point E to P value is formed and crystallizes as consumable output at C, from P to C value is conserved and realized at point C, all the while increasing the entropy of the throughput. At the point of consumption, value sheds its material form and returns to the capitalist as money (M'), while the elements of the material flow are used and flow toward the point of social dissipation or waste.

In Figure 5.4, the path from C to W bears the name "capitalist" waste process, because the process of social dissipation is not reducible to the process of biophysical or entropic dissipation (thus the sloped curve) and in the case of single use commodities such as wrapping could even fall into disuse without any actual physical degradation. Social dissipation or disqualification of matter as useful, or waste, thus supersedes and subsumes the process of physical use and dissipation or disorganization of matter. This differs from the slope of the curve between E and

---

14. In Malm's analysis of fossil capital, this corresponds to CO_2 emissions added at the end of Marx's formula of capital; see Malm, *Fossil Capital*.

P. Because capitalist extraction is founded on very low entropy geological reserves of highly organized matter, fossil fuels in particular, value
is formed faster than entropy, but as the throughput flows through the
process of production, waste accumulates and matter goes through an
irreversible metamorphosis entropic in nature. Between points P and C,
what Marx understood as "circulation," value is conserved but this conservation has a high entropic cost.

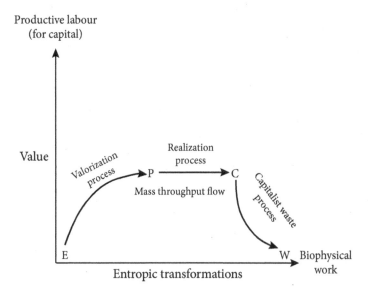

Figure 5.4   The metabolic structure of capitalist accumulation
Source: Author.

Capitalism emerged in the metabolic context of agrarian societies and
it developed into a variety of forms bounded by the limits and constraints
of this metabolic regime. The main determination was an impediment
to unlimited growth because of the specific surplus form, an ecological
surplus that had to be produced. This limited expanded reproduction,
either capital accepted diminishing returns in the agricultural sphere and
those spheres of manufacturing that depended on ecologically mediated
inputs (muscle work and biomass-based materials as well as thermal
energy sources), or it projected itself spatially as merchant, slave trading
and colonial modes of accumulation, including plantation capital. Capi-

talism finds in fossil-industrial metabolism a material basis adequate to its innermost nature, expanded reproduction through the combination of extensive and intensive accumulation dynamics that feed a growth spiral of material flows and monetary claims. In particular, it taps into a biophysical surplus that can drive the machine process, the real subsumption of labor, as well as power that recursively unlocks vast geological reserves of primary materials accompanied by the capacity to transform them productively. Yet this regime is not without its metabolic limits and constraints. In Chapter 4, we identified four such metabolic constraints:

1. source exhaustion or depletion;
2. biophysical limits to efficiency of the machine process;
3. absorption constraint at the point of consumption;
4. sink saturation and ensuing biophysical forcing.

Spurred by its imperative of accumulation, capital has not passively let these constraints limit its growth process. On the contrary, as Marx and many Marxist authors have remarked, capitalism's inherent tendency of development is to transform barriers and limits to its expansion into springboards for renewed cycles of accumulation. That capitalist development is confronted with absolute and unsurpassable biophysical limits today in the form of the climate crisis and biodiversity loss as well as other planetary boundaries does not mean that from the standpoint of capital these appear as unsurmountable.[15] Capital's reaction to metabolic constraints since the origins of the fossil-industrial regime has been to accumulate precisely at those points where these limits and constraints appear. At the dawn of the fossil-fuel age, this meant using coal to extract more coal and overcome the problem of water-saturated mining shafts; today, it takes the form of extreme oil and gas extracted through non-conventional technologies including carbon capture use and storage (CCUS), which implies forcing CO_2 into exploited gas and oil wells to squeeze out more hydrocarbons than otherwise would be available. In a future hoped for by large fossil multinationals such as BP, Shell, Total

15. For a discussion, see Ulrich Brand et al., "From Planetary to Societal Boundaries: An Argument for Collectively Defined Self-Limitation," *Sustainability: Science, Practice and Policy* 17(1) (2021): 264–291, https://doi.org/10.1080/15487733.2021.1 940754.

and ExxonMobil, this could mean producing synthetic hydrogen-based e-fuels from captured atmospheric CO_2, which would prolong throughout this century the specific machine processes and artifacts on which their fixed capital has depended since the early 1900s: fossil fuels and machines powered by internal combustion engines, as well as the social practices of mobility that they mediate.[16] These strategies mobilize capital intensity after a long development of hydrocarbon extraction throughout the twentieth century driven mainly by extensive accumulation dynamics. This switch to what socio-ecological movements have named extreme hydrocarbons transforms the contradictions and conflictual dynamics that arise along these extractive frontiers.[17] Exploring how accumulation frontiers emerge along source and sink limits is a project unto itself, though building on this work, it would need a more elaborated and specific theoretical framework.

More important to our argument here is how capital attempts to surpass the limits that arise around productive and consumptive moments of the throughput flow—problems classically discussed as the contradictions that arise from the moment of valorization and from the moment of realization of value. The Great Acceleration is the outcome of capital's attempt to surpass and overcome the constraints and limits that arise at the point of consumption and manifest themselves as the "absorption constraint" of the produced output. To explore this phenomenon requires moving beyond Marx and adopting an analytical framework that can explain a trajectory of accumulation spurred by the constraint to absorb the very economic surplus capitalism constantly generates at an ever-larger scale. This is precisely the problem that preoccupied the political economists who contributed to the development of a theory of monopoly capital in the mid-twentieth century. The next chapter will draw on their work to complete the model of the drivers of capitalist metabolism in the Great Acceleration.

---

16. See Falko Ueckerdt et al., "Potential and Risks of Hydrogen-Based E-Fuels in Climate Change Mitigation," *Nature Climate Change* 11 (2021): 384–393, https://doi.org/10.1038/s41558-021-01032-7.

17. Éric Pineault, "The Capitalist Pressure to Extract: The Ecological and Political Economy of Extreme Oil in Canada," *Studies in Political Economy* 99(2) (2018): 130–150, https://doi.org/10.1080/07078552.2018.1492063.

6

Accumulation and Social Metabolism in the Great Capitalist Acceleration

The model of accumulation outlined in Chapter 5, based on Marx's insights, has given us a rough picture of the capitalist metabolic regime which mediated fossil fuels and geological sources of matter that emerged in the nineteenth century. As seen in Chapter 4, the metabolic trajectory of capitalist societies is marked by a dramatic shift in growth dynamics after 1950. Most of the variables that express and represent different material aspects of the economic process of capitalist society shift from linear and progressive to exponential and sometimes hyperbolic growth patterns after 1950, thus the "Great Acceleration." The question then is what drove this acceleration? Or, more precisely, the question we will examine here is what socio-ecological changes in capitalist accumulation brought about this acceleration?

As capitalism evolved in the early twentieth century toward a monopolistic form dominated by the large corporation, critical political economy's analysis of capitalist accumulation tended to shift from a focus on valorization (the production of exchange value in the labor process subsumed by capital) to a study of the process of realization of produced value in circulation. This shift implied an analysis of the actual capacity of a monetary economy to validate the prospective profits of firms by the effective absorption of exchange value bearing commodities and the capitalist capture of the ensuing monetary income.[1] Overproduction for Marx was a determining macroeconomic feature of capitalist development which, in the model presented at the end of Book I of *Capital*, would push the accumulation dynamic to a breaking point through suc-

---

1. John Bellamy Foster, *The Theory of Monopoly Capitalism: An Elaboration of Marxian Political Economy*. New York: Monthly Review Press, 2014.

cessive crisis. By the 1900s, it had become apparent to Marxists (Lenin, Luxemburg and Hilferding, for example) and other critical economists, such as Veblen, that giant monopolistic corporations and the holdings or cartels that bound them together, were able to mitigate overproduction/ underconsumption crises to a certain degree, by, for example, limiting the output to what the market could absorb through planned unused capacity.

Thorstein Veblen, in his *The Theory of Business Enterprise* (1904), also understood that the organizational power inherent to the burgeoning corporate form of the capitalist firm had further potential that would prove decisive for the future of capitalism; it would give advanced capitalism a distinctive socio-metabolic growth pattern. Capitalist corporations, in contradistinction to Marx's bourgeois capitalist, rapidly learned to apply their organizational capacity to manage two of the four structural limits discussed in Chapter 5: the biophysical limits of the machine process, or the valorization process; and the absorption limit inherent to the realization process. Capitalist firms reacted to the biophysical limits of the machine process—technological efficiency—by sinking capital into ever-more complex and productive (from the standpoint of capital) machines and industrial systems, a dynamic Marx studied extensively in the third part of *Capital* on relative surplus value. The problem for capital of this inherently dynamic process was that one capitalist's breakthrough was another capitalist's nightmare, as the capital fixed in a productive system with its ensemble of productive artifacts and labor practices as well as the necessary flows of material inputs was suddenly or progressively devalorized. Fixed capital faced a constant and implacable process of devalorization. Spurred by intensive accumulation and the race to capture ever-more relative surplus value, the rotation time of capital lengthened because it was being fixed into ever-larger, more complex machines and production systems, dependent on ever-more massive throughput inflows; the competitive pressure on these rigid structures of accumulation became untenable. Yet, instead of pushing capitalism to its breaking point, it pushed capitalists toward institutional innovations in social property relations and in the organization of the accumulation process to mitigate the constant devaluation of the capital fixed in particularized production processes. This is what both Veblen and Hilferding observed, though they drew very different conclusions on the implications for the future of capitalism. The monopoly capital school on which our analysis is built chose to follow Veblen's intuitions and took seriously the institutional mutation of capitalist property relations that gave birth to the corporate form as "capital embodied."

Devalorization, the central and progressive mechanism in Marx's model of intensive accumulation, rested on the power of the market to sanction capitalist firms according to their differential productivity. With their ascendance to a dominant market position, monopolistic corporations could actively invest in organizational processes that attenuated this sanctioning power. They could shield fixed capital from disruptive innovations either by blocking their introduction through the patent system or by channeling the innovation process so that it took a direction compatible with their fixed productive capacity. Though they were not able to eliminate competition altogether, its form and function did change profoundly as the structures of what would be called "monopolistic competition" settled into an instituted system. This institutional development significantly transformed the accumulation process. Extensive accumulation, constantly faced with the specter of over-investment in redundant productive capacity, incorporated the *planned management* of excess capacity. Intensive accumulation was reworked around the *planned introduction* of potentially disruptive innovations. This was combined with the protection of long-lived rent-generating artifacts as fixed capital assets through patents and the buying out of potentially disruptive start-ups.

The management of devalorization, as much as the race for productivity-enhancing innovation, became a central aspect of the planning process of capitalist enterprise. For Paul Baran, working in the mid-1960s on what would become an unpublished theoretical chapter of *Monopoly Capital*, advanced that capitalism had entered a phase where the central economic problem was not the generation of a valued surplus.[2] The problem for capitalism was how to absorb that valued surplus. Paradoxically, the investment in the organizational capacity to manage excess capacity and innovation further contributed to the rise of the valued surplus at a macroeconomic scale. This became the main driver of the throughput process.

---

2. Paul A. Baran and Paul M. Sweezy, "Some Theoretical Implications," edited by John Bellamy Foster, *Monthly Review*, July 1, 2012, https://monthlyreview.org/2012/07/01/some-theoretical-implications/.

Allan Schnaiberg drew on this theoretical corpus and in the early 1980s proposed the "Treadmill of Production" model to explain the particular growth dynamics of advanced capitalism after 1950. His Treadmill of Production is a "schematic device" that explains "why production expands, why monopoly capital expands its share of production over time, and why production becomes increasingly capital-intensive."[3] The Treadmill of Production model is of interest because it has a strong environmental component, though it is not a model of capitalist *metabolism* per se, it does take into account throughput elements as well as roots the economic process in "environmental withdrawals and additions," sources and sinks. Because it proposed a strong structural explanation of the growth process during the Great Acceleration, the Treadmill of Production model was a dominant theory in English-language environmental sociology all through the 1980s but since then, it has almost disappeared from scientific literature. Its marginalization was not so much caused by sustained critique as by fashion. As sustainable development became a central policy and scientific paradigm, the rather pessimistic approach developed by Schnaiberg was abandoned in favor of more optimistic theories of ecological modernization.[4]

THE TREADMILL OF PRODUCTION MODEL REVISITED

Drawing on the earlier theories of monopoly or oligopolistic capitalism outlined earlier (Kalecki, Baran and Sweezy, Steindl, Eichner), Schnaiberg's model of an advanced capitalist economy is built on the fundamental Marxian class separation between capital and labor, with the vast majority belonging to labor and product market dependent classes. This wide swathe of working classes and middle classes depend on employment both as a means to express their productive and creative capacity as laborers as well as a means to earn the monetary income with which they

3. Allan Schnaiberg, *The Environment: From Surplus to Scarcity*. New York: Oxford University Press, 1980, 227.
4. After almost four decades of normalized environmental policies and politics, as well as a wide adoption of sustainable development goals, objectives, visions and strategies by private organizations have failed to mitigate a growing ecological crisis on a planetary scale. The epistemic positions between these pessimistic and optimistic approaches seems to be moving and interest in the Treadmill of Production model has grown.

must cover their subsistence needs and "consumptive wants." In short, employment is the social institution that mediates the relationship of the vast majority to production and to consumption. For Schnaiberg, writing in the 1970s before the decomposition of the Fordist accumulation regime, there still exists "small-scale entrepreneurialism" as well as subsistence producers, but these are deemed marginal class positions, both socially and economically.[5] Product and labor markets are dominated by large monopolistic capitalist organizations. Labor market dependance means selling one's labor to monopolistic corporations. Product market dependance means buying consumption goods and services that were produced by these same large monopolistic corporations.[6]

The capitalist function in Schnaiberg's model is embodied in large, complex private corporations, controlled by an elite stratum of profit dependent managers and owners/rentiers—in contrast to wage-dependent workers. The important aspect here is that it is the corporate organization, as an organization, which accumulates capital and owns the "means of production." The relationship of the capitalist elite to the accumulation process is mediated by their relation to the corporate organization as a distinct entity—a legal person. This is a fundamental institutional property of advanced capitalist economies that sets them apart from market economies.

Schnaiberg explains that market economies, which fascinated neo-classical economists, are characterized by a tendency toward equilibrium as a myriad of small price-*taking* producer/consumers interact in competitive markets. Advanced capitalist economies are dominated by large price-*making* organizations who develop through the markets (both for inputs and outputs) they control and monopolize, by imposing prices and output quality on price-taking consumers and smaller firms. The degree

---

5. Schnaiberg's Treadmill of Production is thus very "global north" centric and ignores the "edge" position of a large majority of the global working classes, dispossessed yet partial and causing precarity in the relation to both product and labor markets. On this, see Gargi Bhattacharyya's *Rethinking Racial Capital: Questions of Reproduction and Survival*. London: Rowman and Littlefield, 2018.
6. This dependance could be offset by public employment and the production of public goods and services, but Schnaiberg noted that the development of the public economic sector was constrained because its growth decreases the proportion of goods and services in the overall economic output, out of which capitalist firms can draw their profits. This would thus be actively resisted by the profit-dependent capitalist classes.

of control over their environments, through scale and scope, is a function of their size. In the Treadmill of Production model, corporations seek to grow as organizations, but moreover are compelled to grow at least as fast as the economy in which they deploy their capital, lest they lose control over this environment to other competing monopolists or to the state.

In the Treadmill of Production, capitalist growth is only possible through investment and investment is financed from profits. The accumulation of profits is the means through which corporations can grow. Furthermore, given important sunk costs tied to the organizational and material complexity of these producers, a minimum level of production is needed to cover indirect costs before profits can be accumulated. There is thus a high level of inertia or lock-in effects in an economy dominated by large corporations where production, and implied throughput flows, will in a sense be maintained for their own sake to cover indirect costs. This is all the more so given that a significant proportion of these costs are the wages of the elite who exercise managerial control over the corporation and of the white- and pink-collar bureaucracy through which this control is enacted. This is one manifestation of the Treadmill of Production, but there is a deeper and more fundamental force that Schnaiberg sees at work in a capitalist economy dominated by monopolistic corporations. This deeper Treadmill of Production logic appears when we shift our attention from production to accumulation.

Following Marx's theory of expanded reproduction, Schnaiberg posits that growth—understood as the expansion of production controlled by monopolist corporations—is biased toward increased capital intensity (K), or put another way, lower direct labor costs (L) for each unit of output produced and consumed. This classical observation means that investment will speed up the treadmill all the while employing less direct labor. Schnaiberg considers this to be a secular trend of advanced capitalism, profits are captured by higher technology—labor-saving-based production techniques, which increase the *apparent* productivity of labor, all the while not necessarily changing throughput variables: energy and materials. This is a key aspect of Schnaiberg's ecological critique of the treadmill: "In general, increasing the speed of the treadmill involves increased environmental withdrawals and additions." Schnaiberg does admit that "capital intensification of production may lead to more efficient production techniques" but argues that the substitution effects are often not environmentally positive, as in the case of plastic displacing biophysically simpler materials such as wood and metal. Overall "the faster the treadmill is moving [...] the greater the production and environmental impact per worker."[7]

With these characteristics in place, Schnaiberg can then model the dynamics that sets the capitalist treadmill spinning at an accelerating rate:

1. monopoly capitalism directs profits to increased investment in capital intensity or "high technology," this implies decreased labor input per unit produced or inversely increased labor productivity;
2. Increasing capital (K) to labor (L) ratio creates social pressure to expand production to provide employment;
3. Expanded production increases profits, concentrated among the largest firms;
4. Increased volumes of profit are allocated to technological change aimed at increasing capitalization of production;
5. Resulting expanded production must be absorbed by consumers.

"Such expanded consumption merely continues the process [...] above, and frequently accelerates it. This is the essence of the Treadmill, since consumption must increase at ever faster rates to offset the substitution of capital for labor in the production process."[8]

Point number 2 of Schnaiberg's argument merits a closer examination, because it is not self-evident. Where does the pressure to provide employment come from? One could argue that it is a macroeconomic necessity: there is an implicit need for the aggregate volume of wage income to be sufficiently high to validate current expanding production in advanced capitalism. Yet a functional necessity is not an outcome; in a conflictual social form such as capitalism, the absence of a validating volume of wages is a more probable outcome than its existence. Regulation Theory (Aglietta) would explain how this came about through the Fordist class struggle. Schnaiberg, unaware of Aglietta's magnus opus when he wrote on the Treadmill of Production, introduces the socio-political concept of "Growth coalitions" as hegemonic social forces in advanced capitalist societies. Comprising the triad of organized business, organized labor and the interventionist state, he posits that these collective social forces

---

7. Schnaiberg, *The Environment*, 229.
8. Schnaiberg, *The Environment*, 229.

above and beyond their conflicting interests, will each find in economic growth both a means to further their economic means (more profits, more wages, more taxes) and ends (capital accumulation, higher standard of living, stronger economy). This common commitment to growth as means and end translates into a "pressure to provide employment."

Point number 5 has important implications for a class theory of the Great Acceleration. In the original Treadmill of Production model, Schnaiberg insists on the socio-economic mechanisms that create a framework for a "consumer culture" geared toward surplus absorption. It must be noted that as production expands, it meets final demand constraints, overproduction and underconsumption of the potential output are the barriers that the Treadmill must constantly overcome. This leads large corporations to commit significant economic resources (material and symbolic) to the reproduction of a consumer culture, what Regulation Theory has called a consumption norm. In analyzing the limits of consumer sovereignty in shaping the composition of the output through market-based decisions, Schnaiberg examines the contours of this norm and how it is reproduced. The consumption norm is not defined by a standardized basket of commodities for subsistence or prestige purposes, it is rather defined as a particular subjective disposition toward subsistence and prestige goods and services (so-called positional goods), a disposition based on the naturalization of the expansive character of wants, the positive valuation of newness and a high tolerance for various forms of obsolescence including single use commodities. This is further reflected in a shift of class identity among wage laborers as it progressively is redefined around consumptive capacity, living-standards and securing or growing wage-based purchasing-power. Finally, observes Schnaiberg, the "treadmill appears to accelerate more quickly when basic needs are met, and more discretionary income is available for non-necessities."[9]

ADVANCED CAPITALISMS GROWTH DRIVERS AND THEIR METABOLIC IMPLICATIONS

Building on the insights of the Treadmill of Production model, we have a more complete mode of the institutional structure of accumulation in advanced capitalism. Accumulation is not in the hands of individual

---

9. Schnaiberg, *The Environment*, 231.

capitalists; they have been superseded by large integrated and often multinational corporate organizations. These social institutions—literally embodied capital—have their own specific growth drivers tied to their monopolistic nature and it is these that have steered the metabolic process of exponential throughput and stock accumulation growth. A corporation accumulates not only through the output it produces and profits from selling at the highest possible price and producing at the lowest possible cost, which are the parameters of the valorization process we have outlined earlier, it accumulates by actively controlling its economic environment, managing its suppliers, making its markets, determining the demand for its output and fashioning this output of goods and services in such a way as to control and maximize the rate at which they will enter the waste stream. In their seminal work *Monopoly Capitalism*, Paul Baran and Paul Sweezy argued that one of the specific differences of advanced capitalism, namely from Marx's model of competitive capitalism, was that in the former valorization and realization were fused together through the "interpenetration of production and circulation." This means that corporations do not first set out to produce an optimal amount of output and then deploy the efforts to realize this value by selling their products on the market; the "sales effort" regulates *ex-ante* the output form and volume of goods and services to be sold. So if corporations fix large amounts of capital into long-lived productive assets, materialized in a stock–flow–labor nexus organized according to the logic of the machine process, they also fix capital into rent-generating fixed intangible assets such as patents, R-D, trademarks and brands and other forms of intellectual property.[10] And if the laboring masses tied to some of the largest corporations can be counted in hundreds of thousands, a significant proportion of these workers are not direct producers of goods and services; they produce the organizational power of the corporation. The product of their labor is information, communication, measure, coordination and control. We can consider all these forms of control as one generic and abstract form: the accumulation of capitalist organizational power over society, over social metabolism and social relations to nature as well as social reproduction.

---

10.   To this must be added the immense value of capital fixed in electronic platforms which monopolize the flow of information and goods on the internet.

This gives growth in an advanced capitalist economy a determined form and content. Above and beyond—or rather through growth as measured by GDP: more commodified goods and services per person, per labor hour, or per dollar invested, and as measured by the material throughput, growth is also more social relations of production, consumption and reproduction, more experiences and more social relations to nature mediated by the organizational capacity of corporate capital—their real subsumption by capital. The vast accumulation of material stocks in the last 70 years noted as a distinctive characteristic of fossil-industrial metabolism, and discussed in Chapters 1 and 4, are instruments of this subsumption. The production, accumulation and diffusion of artifacts and infrastructures built and manufactured out of geological stocks by monopolistic corporations is an essential foundation of the capacity to mediate and subsume socio-ecological practices. In previous chapters, we examined these artifacts as elements of the stock flow practice nexus in the abstract; here, we see that artifacts always exist in institutionalized social property relations and this determines the way they will mediate social practice.

CAPITALIZED AND COMMODIFIED STOCKS AND FLOWS

Artifacts can exist as "capitalized assets" or fixed capital that mediate productive, extractive, distributive and dissipative processes and social practice as labor in the spheres of production, extraction and waste. Corporate capital can be divided among six asset forms, listed from the least to the most liquid forms.

1. engineered works (infrastructures such as hydro-electric dams, deep-sea drilling platforms, mines)
2. buildings
3. machinery and materials
4. intellectual property and intangibles
5. financial assets
6. money

The first four asset forms correspond to investment in productive capital accumulation, whereas the last two forms correspond to savings and financial forms of investment more speculative in nature. In mature advanced capitalist economies, investment is often equally spread across the four productive forms.

Three of these asset forms exist as artifacts: engineered works, buildings and machinery. On the one hand, as stocks, they have a determining impact on flows and, on the other hand, as capitalized assets, their existence and use are determined by the accumulation strategy of capitalist firms. And because capitalist extraction, production and dissipation are mediated by labor—even in machine process dominated systems—workers, the labor movement and the state are also among the forces that impact the use, creation and destruction of artifacts and thus the mass flows they will govern. The growth coalition form outlined by Schnaiberg does not only concern the economy as a whole, but it can also emerge as a decisive force around certain key artifacts as debates around "Just transition" and the phasing out of coal or other hydrocarbons have shown. But overall, the daily management by monopolistic corporations of the devalorization of fixed capital and the constraint they face to keep fixed capital working (extracting transforming, circulating, dissipating) to recover sunk costs are the hegemonic forces that mediate the stock–flow–practice nexus built around productive capitalized artifacts. And the longer-term accumulation strategies adopted by these firms in terms of sectors and emphasis between extensive and intensive approaches govern the growth pattern of the "productive" fraction of material stocks. In terms of ecological impact of these material stocks (for example in the form of GHG emissions), the extraction, production and dissipative relations they mediate, their operation and use, the output they generate and its throughput, is much more serious than the impact derived from their construction. The ecological impact of investment in fixed capital assets must be considered in view of the long-term implications of the added quantity of productive stocks and the future throughput flows they command (this is why many anti-fossil-fuel campaigns attack pipeline projects instead of occupying and disrupting sites of extraction such as wells and pits).

Capitalized assets are also essential to the mediation of consumptive practices at the point of juncture between production and consumption where artifacts, built infrastructure and buildings mediate the acquisition of goods and services as capitalist systems of provisioning. And in doing so they also mediate social activity as labor for those workers who service the provisioning systems.

Artifacts also exist as durable and semi-durable goods that mediate reproductive practices, artifacts produced and designed by corporate capital but accumulated as owned stocks by households and individuals for consumptive purposes.[11] Though purposefully designed to be unproductive, these artifacts mediate mass flows of matter and energy as they are used. Their use, the way they subsume reproductive practices and social activity in general, aims to transform these practices into an activity that becomes dependent on commodified artifacts and dependent on commodified flows of matter and energy. In the history of their development during the Great Acceleration, the machine process gradually and inexorably became the defining principle of their being, from power tools to electric toothbrushes to the automobile and washing machine, engines became core features of automated functioning to which is being added today computers and internet interfaces that plug each artifact as a node into a corporately controlled system of communication and information. And, of course, all this takes ever-more energy.

As simple an operation as whisking an egg, which once involved a hen and its feed, a bowl and a wooden or metal tool, now involves fossil-fuel-subsidized industrial agriculture, a refrigeration machine complete with tactile screen and internet connection, and a plastic molded cheaply built powered whisk with a useful life of two years or less, and electricity to power the fridge, the whisk and eventually the dishwasher to clean up afterwards. Leaf blowers take this development to the extreme, knowing that humanity has raked with almost the same type of tool for at least the last 7,000 years and it is only in the last decade that this ancient and simple but efficient extension of our capacity to grasp has been replaced by gas-guzzling and inefficient air-blowing machines (with a design that has a vague resemblance to a hand-held rocket launcher, this probably helps selling the product to men).

---

11. Residential structures are a more complex affair. Some being privately held, others are corporately owned, and both are capitalized financially but not productively. Unproductivity is built in to their material form or imposed through institutions such as zoning rules. They have longer lifespans as stocks, but the command they exercise over flows is considerable, both material and energetic, and finally, they are designed and used as a "site" of consumption of other commodified artifacts and flows.

The distinction between productive and unproductive[12]—but reproductive—artifacts is also one between *capitalization*[13] and *commodification* as the principle that organizes the social property relations, use and material being and form of the stocks. This means it also defines the way these stocks will determine and regulate flows. Because they are commodified instead of capitalized, the founding principle of these stocks is an inverse relation to time and use. Corporations seek to prolong the useful life of capitalized artifacts and reduce as much as possible turnover rates but seek to shorten as much as possible the useful life of commodified artifacts and grow turnover rates. Producing corporations must build and design these objects according to a planned and optimized churn rate (for example, cellphone manufacturers typically aim for a two-year churn rate), a principle streamlined by General Motors in the 1920s for automobiles. The *point de fuite* and bliss point of commodity producers is the combination of a single-use disposable artifact and an adopted and reinforced habitual use or practice.

Early social experiments with this commodity form were the first disposable razor blades. In the twenty-first century, this artifact form has become pervasive and with the advent of personal electronic devices—invasive. The metabolic consequences of this object-form are many. Of course, they themselves flow from source to sink and thus high churn rates and growth of their stocks through functional diversification—more objects per household to do more things—and massification—more

---

12. In advanced capitalism, this division is actually an interesting dialectic tied to the imperative of realization of value. In their sales effort to households, corporations will actively play with this boundary through "transgressive" marketing ploys. Do-it-yourself culture is one example, but a more spectacular example with more serious environmental consequences is the SUV and the pick-up truck. Power and utility, the capacity to work is what distinguishes the marketing effort and design of these vehicles from classic sedans and smaller compacts. Yet, in the authors experience, actually trying to use most of these vehicles to do "useful work" other than transporting humans on paved roads is actually dangerous, and using them for their bulk transport capacity is inefficient (I also had a similar experience with a consumer versus a commercial chainsaw). In the end, what is an SUV? A signifier and a means to absorb per vehicle sold a greater mass of extracted metals, produced plastics and refined oil than if one produced a simple compact vehicle with a fuel-efficient operation in mind. On the wider "political ecology of the SUV," see Ulrich Brand and Markus Wissen, *The Imperial Mode of Living*, Chapter 6.

13. Capital goods such as machinery, engineered works and buildings can exist as commodities, but most are made to order and have a very weak degree of liquidity, thus, the expression "fixed" capital.

equal distribution or access to these objects among income groups and along the North–South divide—have important quantitative and qualitative impacts on extraction and dissipation: from the explosive growth of mining activities for rare and critical metals to the mass circulation of e-waste from North to South. But these artifacts, even the most short-lived, often command flows themselves when they mediate social practices—energy flows in particular. The massive energy demand of internet activity mediated by various e-devices has become a reality energy provisioning systems have to cope with.

And finally they exist as public and private infrastructures, buildings and artifacts which are consumed collectively such as shopping malls, cinemas and entertainment parks, that sustain social reproduction in ways that are not subsumed by capital as consumption (think of water provisioning and waste-water collection and treatment infrastructure or public libraries) or support and mediate practices of mobility and circulation—roads, bridges, railways, ports and canals, public transit systems and airports. Capital owns the first, produces the second and through neoliberal policies its logic has progressively permeated the latter, which it builds and increasingly operates at profit. Finally, the point of dissipation is also structured by artifacts that mediate social practices of waste, making those designed into consumed durable and semi-durable artifacts as well as in single-use commodities that we explored earlier. This design effort corresponds to intangible assets accumulated by corporations as

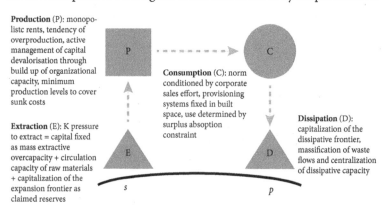

Production (P): monopolistc rents, tendency of overproduction, active management of capital devalorisation through build up of organizational capacity, minimum production levels to cover sunk costs

Consumption (C): norm conditioned by corporate sales effort, provisioning systems fixed in built space, use determined by surplus absoption constraint

Extraction (E): K pressure to extract = capital fixed as mass extractive overcapacity + circulation capacity of raw materials + capitalization of the expansion frontier as claimed reserves

Dissipation (D): capitalization of the dissipative frontier, massification of waste flows and centralization of dissipative capacity

Figure 6.1   Capitalist determination of the throughput
Source: Author.

well as machine-based systems of waste disposal and management that require labor and are often nested in capitalist–corporate social relations of property.[14] The specific capitalist relations to these artifacts not only mediate social practice, but they also imply a capitalist regulation of the throughput flow governed by these artifacts according to the principles laid out in Chapter 1.

Figure 6.1 summarizes the capitalist determination of material stocks and flows along the throughput and how this mediates the accumulation process.

GROWTH IMPETUS AND GROWTH IMPERATIVE, DRIVING THE THROUGHPUT AND ACCUMULATION

The forces that drive the growth process in advanced capitalism—and on which is based its particular logic of accumulation—are, on the one hand, a growth *impetus* and, on the other hand, a growth *imperative*. Examining these driving forces, we summarize and synthesize elements from both the Marxian and Treadmill approach to growth and metabolism we have been working with.

The impetus for growth in advanced capitalism originates from the profits that capitalist organizations accumulate. In a monopolistic economy, profits tend to gravitate toward the largest corporations, giving them the opportunity to invest in the expansion of their activities at the expense of other, smaller, less powerful businesses. But the other side of this is that the larger an organization, the more it will have to invest to control the scope of its economic activity given that both its internal and external environment have grown. This will result in a pressure large corporations feel to maximize their growth rates.[15] Doing so implies maximizing the output of produced goods and services to as much as the market can absorb, and this in turn implies building up surplus productive capacity. Corporations will thus sink a significant amount of retained profits into long-lived, fixed capital assets, tangible and intangible, that

14. Michael Dawson, *The Consumer Trap: Big Business Marketing in American Life.* Champaign, IL: University of Illinois Press, 2005.
15. Alfred S. Eichner, *The Megacorp and Oligopoly: Micro Foundations of Macro Dynamics.* Cambridge: Cambridge University Press, 1976; and Marc Lavoie, *Post-Keynesian Economics: New Foundations.* Cheltenham: Edward Elgar, 2022, https://doi.org/10.4337/9781839109621.

can produce these goods and services. But they will not passively let the market determine how much of their surplus will be absorbed; they will invest in the capacity to control, shape and define through organizational capacity the production and consumption regimes of these goods and services, to control demand and supply. As we saw earlier, this mode of accumulation has been called "extensive" in the sense that it is based on growing current productive and consumption patterns as they exist. And with them will also grow the volume of the throughput.

But corporations are also constantly plowing profits into the capacity to innovate and this, as we saw in a Marxian perspective, has paradoxical implications. On the one hand, an innovative corporation can literally "make its market" and enjoy, for a limited period, a monopoly position and high economic rents. But on the other hand, innovation, be it in the productive or consumption regime, will destroy the value of some fixed capital assets, which suddenly become unproductive (think automation), or which produce an output that no one desires (think tape recorders). The introduction of new technologies, new goods and services, new needs and wants is a planned and organized process in capitalism where each corporation seeks to manage the devalorization of its fixed capital assets. This "intensive" mode of accumulation changes the composition of the throughput and the resulting growth has important ecological and biophysical consequences. Because extractive and externalization processes are themselves highly capitalized and organized through corporate power in this type of capitalist economy, throughput is "cheap"—to use an expression by Jason Moore.[16] Because of rebound effects, more efficient artifacts from a biophysical perspective will actually grow rather than shrink the throughput. And finally, more complex and smart artifacts require more diverse and complex materials with more potentially toxic components. So above and beyond the rhetoric of sustainability, corporate innovations in the productive and consumptive spheres will result in a metabolism that is more biophysically intense and ecologically destructive, rather than less.

---

16.   But in a manner here that is the exact opposite of his all-encompassing and transhistorical "law" of the tendency of the ecological surplus to fall. Here the argument is that in the specific historical context of advanced capitalism, throughput is cheap because it is capitalized, not because it isn't. This follows Wrigley's rule outlined in Chapter 4; see E.A. Wrigley, *Energy and the English Industrial Revolution*. Cambridge: Cambridge University Press, 2010.

Be it extensive or intensive, in both cases, growth will result as a combination of expanded output, expanded productive capacity and expanded consumption of this output. Each and every corporation will maximize its growth rate to expand the control over its environment, its output and the rate of change of both, knowing its competitors are doing the same. The result is a corporate growth *imperative*. If a given corporation does not maximize its growth rate, it will lose monopoly power, profit share and eventually the capacity to maintain its relative control over those economic relations of production and consumption through which it accumulates. And thus, the imperative of growth that each and every corporation faces is the spur that drives the overall accumulation rate of a capitalist monetary production economy. This accumulation will drive the biophysical processes in the economy, the accumulation of throughput hungry stocks and the acceleration of the throughput fashioned output of commodified goods and services.

THE SOCIAL ECOLOGY OF CAPITALIST METABOLISM: A SUMMARY OF THE ARGUMENT AND ITS ECOLOGICAL CONSEQUENCES

Capitalist growth exists both as the expansion of the monetary production economy and as the upscaling of social metabolism. The former is adequately captured and measured by GDP, the latter by the physical units that make up the throughput needed to maintain a given set of stocks of artifacts and living beings. Scale is the combination of both phenomena—aspects of the same reality. When one is put in motion, the other will be moved. So, when a capitalist spends money in the productive sphere or extractive sphere, labor will move, direct and control tools and machines, output in the form of raw materials and goods and services will result. But labor can only move, direct and control machines if they are fed with the appropriate throughput of energy and matter. Furthermore, machines need a constant inflow of matter to maintain their productive capacity as they breakdown and parts have to be replaced or refurbished. Finally, material flows also expand as the monetary production economy expands, matter accumulates as a growing stock of new machines, which will need larger throughputs of energy and matter. We have measured, analyzed and examined this metabolic process throughout this work. For the social ecology of capital, the Marxian capital and labor relation of exploitation does not exist in isolation; it exists in a material world of energy and matter flows, biophysical and ecological mediations of the accumulation and ensuing economic process. For labor to work, for fixed capital to accumulate, for the output to grow, a throughput must be extracted, put to work and eventually dissipated and absorbed by ecological and biogeochemical sinks. At the end of this analytical journey, we can summarize our findings as the following four implications for an understanding of the metabolic dimension of capitalism:

1. Relations of production always imply bundles of fixed capital (K), labor (L), energy (E) and materials (M) in determined forms and quantities which mediate each other in the capitalist machine process. This means that a given unit of labor time, or a given unit of output in goods and services always implies a given unit of energy and matter in a determined form. Energy and matter that must be extracted, that will be transformed and that will be absorbed in sinks, forcing to some degree ecosystems and biogeochemical cycles. These KLEM ratios are bundled into the *form* of the stock of the productive artifacts of a capitalist society through investment decisions. In an advanced capitalist economy, investment decisions are primarily controlled by large corporations and financed through the sale of debt instruments on centralized markets. This results in a capitalist "lock-in" of KLEM ratios in long-lived, privately controlled productive artifacts that must generate a return on investment, not only for the firm but also for those who own an income claim on the artifact through financial instruments. The consumption process also implies bundles which are similar to KLEM but the artifacts that populate households are not subject to a capitalist valorization process, they are commodified in lieu of being capitalized. The lock-in rests rather on a different imperative: artifacts will be designed according to marketing principles so that their obsolescence can be controlled by the corporate sector and demand conditioned. KLEM ratios thus govern the biophysical throughput of the economic process.

2. This throughput is subject to the Entropy Law which implies that as matter and energy flow through the economy, they are irreversibly transformed and biophysically degraded. Once felled, a tree can be cut into squared lumber, and from squared lumber one can

construct a wooden table. During this process, a certain proportion of the wood contained in the tree will be lost as sawdust, and the energy expended in the forming and shaping of the components of the table will be lost as heat. One cannot reverse the process and create a tree out of the table; one could not even transform the table back into the original squared timber. A perfectly circular economy is an impossibility. Of course, once it is decided that the table is "waste," this waste can enter into the labor process as "recycled" matter or energy (if burnt to heat a forge, for example), but this new transformation will imply a net input of matter and energy into the throughput, and thus more extraction and more absorption of waste in sinks, and thus potentially additional ecological and bio-geochemical forcing depending on the KLEM ratios. The only means by which the throughput and ecological and biogeochemical forcing can be reduced significantly is by the production of long-lived, labor-intensive and largely passive artifacts. But the output in capitalism develops in precisely the opposite manner: goods and services tend to be short-lived (smart phones) energy intensive (air travel), labor-saving (leaf blowers), material intensive (plastic packaging). Why? Because it is this high turnover output that guar-antees growth of profits in the advanced capitalist treadmill.

3. The scale of the throughput then, other things being equal, is a function of the nature and size of the stocks of capitalized and commodified artifacts that are built up in the monetary produc-tion economy. In an advanced capitalist economy, this stock is disproportionately owned as fixed capital by large monopolistic corporations and thus subject to a valorization imperative. This means that in such an economy this imperative governs the scale of the throughput and the impacts of its ecological and biogeochemi-cal forcing. Moreover, corporations will exercise what social power they can muster to protect these long-lived, capitalized assets from devalorization through innovation or regulation. Competing tech-nologies or products will be bought up, regulators lobbied, a growing throughput rate will be locked in to this economy's trajectory as artifacts are privately accumulated. The only noticeable slowdown of the overall throughput rate corresponds to economically and

socially problematic slowdowns of the rate of accumulation during periods of crisis: recessions and depressions.[17]

4. The relationship between artifacts and throughput flows is relatively fixed in the short term; it can only be changed by investment, which in an advanced capitalist economy is largely in the hands of the large corporations and governed by their private decisional power. KLEM bundles tend to be locked in, as do their ecological consequences. It is commonly assumed that "growth," because it expands the monetary production economy, opens space for investment in new productive artifacts that are "more efficient" and this efficiency can have positive ecological effects, locking in environmentally better KLEM bundles in artifacts. This then leads to the common thesis that growth can somehow be decoupled from biophysical constraints and ecological consequences—a social ecology of capitalist metabolism leads to a rather different set of conclusions. Three economic mechanisms thwart the decoupling process: the rebound effect, the capitalization of extraction and the capitalization of externalization.

The first mechanism has been widely studied by ecological economists. It refers to a situation where efficiency gains translate into higher throughputs of energy or matter because of a wider adoption or more intense use of a given artifact or technology. Another form of rebound is when the efficiency leads to lower costs, which free up income that is then used to consume other goods and services, which then leads to a higher throughput. The capitalization of extraction is based on the fact that in advanced capitalism extractive activity implies very high initial investments in extractive and most importantly in the bulk transport capacity of unprocessed staples. In this structure, it is only at a certain mass scale that flows of extracted matter and energy are economically profitable. Furthermore, the more difficult the biophysical conditions of extraction, the more the process will be capitalized, and the more the flow of commodities must be large to cover sunk costs. This capitalization process generates a steady

---

17. Qinglong Shao, Anke Schaffartzik, Andreas Mayer and Fridolin Krausmann, "The High 'Price' of Dematerialization: A Dynamic Panel Data Analysis of Material Use and Economic Recession," *Journal of Cleaner Production* 167 (2017): 120–132, https://doi.org/10.1016/j.jclepro.2017.08.158.

stream of abundant low-cost, standardized staple commodities, which are "pushed into the capitalist economy" and lock in the use of certain materials and sources of energy, crowding out alternatives. Furthermore, the capital fixed in the extractive infrastructure is large and long lived; the amortization time of these investments can be counted in decades. So, the capitalization of extraction keeps the throughput growing by the "abundance effect" of sunk costs and bulk extraction and circulation.

A similar process can be seen at the sink end of the throughput, in the specific form of a capitalization of the externalization of wastes and eco-logical disruptions. The archetypical form of capitalized externalization is the industrial chimney or the sewer discharging waste and pollution in bodies of water. In either case, capital is fixed in the capacity to direct the end point of the throughput and its ecological effects away from core cap-italist societies and most importantly their elites. And the more efficient the capitalized externalization mechanism, the more the "economy" has room to grow its throughput or maintain a throughput volume that is ecologically unsustainable.

Capitalization, being investment, is a growth strategy through which stocks are accumulated by fixing capital in productive artifacts. The three above-mentioned mechanisms ensure that investment in a capi-talist setting will not result in more ecologically efficient KLEM ratios that could shrink or slow the material throughput. Though there will be some substitution effects, coal will recede, fracked natural gas will take its place, but there is an inherent tendency for the rates to rise or at least be maintained.

Resulting growth in advanced capitalism will thus be experienced:

1. as a growing—capitalistically determined—output or a growing abundance of commodified goods and services.
2. as the continued mediation by large corporations of ever-greater aspects of productive, consumptive and reproductive daily life activity, including reproductive and care activity, as well as metabolic and aesthetic relations to nature. This experience will lead to the acceptance and legitimacy of this mediation by private capital.
3. as the experience of social change in the form of a continuous change in output composition (and the desire for the new) as well

as change in labor experience and consumptive practices (the desire for social acceleration).

4. as accelerating ecological change and disrupted biogeochemical cycles which will be experienced as an imperative to adapt to new, unfamiliar and unstable environmental patterns, which will retroactively act on the conditions of accumulation and social reproduction and spur new growth imperatives.

These are the forces that will shape the metabolism of the capitalist monetary production economy. They will govern the formation of stocks in the form of artifacts that are fixed capital assets held by monopolistic corporations or durable goods such as homes, cars, motor tools and appliances used by households, both having capitalistically determined rates of depreciation. Throughput will flow to feed and renew these stocks, but it will also flow in the coalesced form of shorter-living commodities embodied in goods and services that have a capitalistically determined waste rate. Depreciation rates and waste rates, as well the penetration of commodified goods and services in social life and relations are the means through which corporations can expand their output and organizational control in the race to transform their profits into economic power over society (growth impetus) and maintain their scale and scope in a growing economy (growth imperative). These are the social forces of a deeper treadmill of accumulation that are reflected in the fossil-industrial metabolic regime's drive to a Great Acceleration.

Conclusion
Emancipation Amid the Ruins of Fossil Metabolism

The metabolism of capitalist societies deploys material flows and accumulates material stocks that truly are geological in scale. The yearly mass of matter extracted and put into circulation by capital will soon exceed the biomass produced by all the Earth's terrestrial ecosystems during the same period. The exponential growth that has characterized fossil-industrial metabolism is changing the face of the planet to a point where the basic biogeochemical cycles that shape the Earth system are approaching dangerous tipping points and zones of instability.[1] This has wide and extensive impacts on biodiversity: the viability of the last non-anthropized biomes (the Amazon, the boreal forests) is being undermined, novel artificialized ecosystems—(anthromes) such as pastures, plantations and agro-industrial fields—now cover much of the Earth's emerged surface and they have enhanced the ecological instability of the planet. And finally, the unrelenting emission of greenhouse gases is setting the Earth's climate on a hothouse trajectory with a probable warming of 2 to 4.5 degrees in the next millennium, rendering vast portions of the planet inhabitable for human beings. These are uncontroversial facts accepted by a wide community of natural and social scientists. They appear as a strong consensus in the latest IPCCC reports, their implications are discussed by those debating the existence of an Anthropocene age that has succeeded the Holocene age. Though we can trace the origins of climate change and global warming to the intertwining of the carbon cycle and the fossil-based metabolic regime 200 years ago, the last 70 years has seen the ecological pressures and unsustainable social mediations of the Earth's living cycles intensify in a historical process that has been named the Great

---

1. David I. Armstrong McKay et al., "Exceeding 1.5°C Global Warming Could Trigger Multiple Climate Tipping Points," *Science* 377(6611) (2022), eabn7950, https://doi.org/10.1126/science.abn7950.

Acceleration by Earth scientists and environmental historians. From a social metabolic point of view, the period after 1950 has its own particular throughput and stock accumulation dynamics, both quantitatively—in terms of the unprecedented scale of flows and accumulated artifacts, and qualitatively, in terms of the materialities involved.

We have provided an analytical framework to understand the capitalist nature of this Great Acceleration. Our focus has been on how, in advanced capitalism, overproduction and overconsumption are articulated to each other, how extractive and dissipative processes become in themselves sites of capital accumulation, how these economic relations are instituted as an accumulation regime that reproduces the organizational power of corporate capital as a whole and drives the throughput flow as well as determines how this translates into an accumulation of material stocks. Our argument has been that the power of investment monopolized by corporate capital determines in large part the metabolic structures—the stock–flow–practice nexus—of contemporary societies. This power shapes and defines the four structural moments that make up the economic process from a metabolic perspective: extraction, production, consumption and dissipation of the material throughput. Capital embodied in the organizational power of large corporations accumulates and is fixed in both tangible and intangible forms at each of these points of the throughput and drives its flow. As capital accumulates, the scale of the economic process grows; growth manifests itself both as a macroeconomic process aptly captured by GDP metrics and as a biophysical phenomenon, the metrics of which were extensively explored in Chapter 1. Growth is both a result and an enabling condition of capitalist accumulation, providing an impetus for further accumulation but it exists also as an imperative that the economic surplus must be absorbed by expansion of consumption and investment.

The material foundations of this growth treadmill have been the specific metabolic relations developed by fossil capital based on the mass extraction and transformation of geological sources of matter: fossil fuels, metals and non-metallic minerals, in particular those needed to build concrete structures. Capital has found in fossil energy sources a pre-existing stock that it could almost immediately put to work, in the case of coal and gas, while oil needed some transformation, but crucially, oil could be burnt to extract and refine oil into useful fuels. The fossil-based biophysical surplus has sustained the growth dynamic and accumulation of capital over the last two centuries; it has also powered the worldwide extension of capitalist dynamics and of fossil-industrial metabolism, albeit in unequal and asymmetrical ways.[2] The mobilization of this bio-physical surplus also fundamentally changed the way capitalist societies appropriated biomass through agriculture in particular. For millennia agricultural labor entwined with the organic activity of living beings (plants and animals) in managed ecosystems was the predominant means of producing a biophysical surplus appropriable in social forms. This surplus could further be mobilized as muscle power (animal and human) and put to work to extract precious—from a metabolic perspective—geological sources of matter: metals, hewn stone and minerals. And though these materials were important to agrarian societies, agri-culture, husbandry and forestry produced most of the elements of their material throughput. In the fossil-industrial metabolic regime, the eco-logical structure of agricultural production is inverted, from a source of biophysical surplus, agriculture becomes a material and energetic sink; the organic growth of biomass across vast anthromes the world over has come to depend on fossil-fuel inputs. A telling example is the collapse in 2022 of agricultural productivity in Thailand, after the government banned the import and use of synthetic fertilizers for economic and fiscal reasons tied to the explosion of their costs in the wake of Russia's war with Ukraine.

Agro-ecological production, tying together the potentialities of organic growth of crops with labor and social management of ecological relations of plant communities does subsist, but this complex of socio-metabolic relations that has sustained human societies since the end of the great gla-ciation 10,000 years ago has been severely marginalized. High apparent productivity of fossilized agro-industrial ecosystems has emancipated a significant proportion of society from the constraints and limits of land-based subsistence production. This material emancipation has sustained the development of a deepening and widening social division of labor. This division is not only based on the principles of specialization but also on the functional, existential and geographical separation between extraction, production, consumption and dissipation, unified only from

2. Christoph Görg et al., "Scrutinizing the Great Acceleration: The Anthropocene and its Analytic Challenges for Social–Ecological Transformations," *Anthropocene Review* 7(1) (2019): 42–61, https://doi.org/10.1177/2053019619895034.

the vantage point of capitalist social relations. Adam Smith considered this deepening social division of labor as a wellspring of productivity and potential material abundance—as long as the development of unfettered markets followed in step. For him and liberal thinkers thereafter, the potentiality for social emancipation from want and servitude became tied to a progressive material emancipation from direct subsistence production through the development of an ever-more complex social division of labor.[3] Marx and most socialist thinkers afterwards conserved this same articulation of material emancipation as a premise and condition for social emancipation, but replaced unfettered markets by self-conscious coordination among direct producers, introducing the idea that the development of the modern social division of labor could be socially planned. The perspective of social ecology considers the combustion of fossil fuels, externalization and unequal ecological exchange to be the real material basis on which this modern division of labor has been built.[4]

A central manifestation of this deepened and fossilized division of labor has been the growing concentration of most of humanity in vast urban environments and the adoption of urban modes of life and work based on the socio-metabolic potentialities that these environments offer.[5] Capitalism, as we know it, is intimately tied to the development of urban *lebensweiss* (modes of life). The modern urban form, especially in its sprawled North American variant, has been particularly apt at absorbing the immense surpluses, both biophysical and social, that capitalist production has set in motion during the Great Acceleration. It is on this material base that mass-consumption-based lifestyles, both privileged and precarious, and their modes of subjectivation, have become the norm in advanced capitalist societies.[6] The constraint

3.   Gareth Dale, "Seventeenth Century Origins of the Growth Paradigm," in Iris Borowy and Matthias Schmelzer (eds.), *History of the Future of Economic Growth: Historical Roots of Current Debates on Sustainable Degrowth*. Abingdon: Routledge, 2017, 27–51.

4.   Ulrich Brand and Markus Wissen, *The Imperial Mode of Living: Everyday Life and the Ecological Crisis of Capitalism*. London: Verso, 2021; and Alf Hornborg, *Nature, Society, and Justice in the Anthropocene: Unraveling the Money–Energy–Technology Complex*. Cambridge: Cambridge University Press, 2019.

5.   Murray Bookchin's social ecology developed a fecund and original critique of this process in his opus *Urbanization Without Cities: The Rise and Decline of Citizenship*. Montreal: Black Rose Books, 1992.

6.   Dennis Eversberg, "From Democracy at Others' Expense to Externalization at Democracy's Expense: Property-Based Personhood and Citizenship Struggles in

to produce what one *cannot* consume, while depending on means of consumption that one *cannot* produce—a characteristic of societies with significant divisions of labor—has been pushed to the extreme by the capitalist dynamics of the last decades as global corporations have developed ever-longer, complex and opaque, commodity chains. The vast flows of matter, the scale of extraction and the ensuing scale of dissipation that we have studied and that marks the materiality of contemporary societies has as a parallel the immense store of fossil-fuel reserves that must be combusted yearly to keep the throughput flowing. Finally, it is the very nature of the materialities out of which life worlds are built that have radically changed in the last decades. Fossil-dependent materials such as plastic, energy-intensive metals such as aluminum and titanium, and fossil-dependent infrastructures and buildings of concrete have profoundly changed our social and natural world. As information and communication technologies become mediations of the everyday life for ever-greater swathes of humanity, new rare metals and other energy and land intensive materials enter the throughput flow, exacerbating socio-ecological conflicts around both extractive and dissipative frontiers, be it open-pit graphite mines in the advanced capitalist core or e-waste dumps externalized in peripheries such as Ghana or Southeast Asia.

To break out of this growth treadmill not only must the corporate institution, capitalist property and production relations in general be broken up and unwound, but much of the fixed capital accumulated as machines and fossil-based infrastructures will have to be dismantled and replaced. Habits and modes of living and working, material aspirations and cultures of consumption sustained by intangible capital fixed in design, marketing and advertisement will also have to be challenged and transformed. The Growth Treadmill of modern capitalist society has also a strong political foundation that we have barely examined in this work, but it does require scrutiny from a social ecology standpoint.[7] Growth is a political imperative in a capitalist society; it is a central mechanism of this society's need of the dynamic stabilization of its constituent contra-

Organized and Flexible Capitalism," *Anthropological Theory* 21(3) (2021): 315–340, https://doi.org/10.1177/146349962097799.

7. Melanie Pichler, Anke Schaffartzik, Helmut Haberl and Christoph Görg, "Drivers of Society–Nature Relations in the Anthropocene and Their Implications for Sustainability Transformations," *Current Opinion in Environmental Sustainability* 26–27 (2017): 32–36, https://doi.org/10.1016/j.cosust.2017.01.017.

dictions. This brings us back to Adam Smith. He argued in the *Wealth of Nations* that, in a class society, social conflict between the constituent classes of the emerging modern capitalist society: capitalists, landowners as rentiers (to which we can assimilate financial capital today) and wage earners, could be regulated either by repression and violence or through growth of the output (both solutions are presented in Chapter 8 of the *Wealth of Nations*). In modern capitalist society, class struggle, if it does not challenge existing relations of production, but merely struggles inside these relations—as it does most of the time—is a struggle over the allocation and distribution of the economic surplus. The only way to avoid a zero-sum game, where one's gain is another's loss, is by growing the surplus. This leads to what Allan Schnaiberg named a "growth coalition." This coalition, typical of modern capitalist class societies, is formed of the tryptic: capital, labor and state. Each has a stake in growth and each plays a functional role in the macroeconomics of growth: labor as mass consumers and direct producers; capitalists as investors that direct the expansion of the system; and the state through budgetary, fiscal and trade policies that support and stabilize growth as well as redistribute in a legitimate fashion acquired social rights to wealth. Inside this triangle of relations between state, labor and capital, it is possible to develop a more radical theory of exploitation, showing how in the end all social wealth is produced by workers and they should thus have the full control over relations of production. But it is impossible to see and question the boundary effects of growth that we have studied throughout this work and the socio-ecological contradictions that economic expansion into society and nature imply. On the contrary, given the socio-political growth imperative of capitalist society, it is possible to understand why the constitutive groups of the growth coalition: organized labor, capital and the modern state, will spontaneously converge toward growth-based answers to the ecological contradictions of capitalist expansion. Thus, the need for an autonomous critique of economic scale and of growth as the material expression and manifestation of accumulation.

A truly ecological and just society, from the standpoint examined in this work, must break with much of the materiality and metabolic patterns on which modern capitalism has grown. "Forces of production" developed by capitalism cannot be viewed with hope as instruments which, once socialized, can lay the foundations for a viable emancipatory future. On the contrary, they must be considered with caution and suspicion, as products of a fossil-based metabolism, shaped by the veil of machine fetishism, sustained by asymmetric material flows between center and periphery and externalized ecological impacts. Their development, based on a radical separation and estrangement of production and consumption, undermines and colonizes the everyday unity of reproductive activities: commodifying objects, care and social relations based on commoning. An emancipatory politics today cannot base its vision of "what could be" on the potentialities developed by capitalist accumulation. Furthermore, an emancipatory politics today that takes seriously the materiality of society, and its ecological contradictions, must come to terms with limits to social metabolism. The notion that emancipation from materiality is a precondition for social emancipation must be dropped if limits are to be reflexively and justly instituted by society at global and local scales.

Among the approaches to social emancipation, it would seem that "Degrowth"[8] is the proposition that has examined these questions the most thoroughly (this includes Degrowth-oriented Ecosocialism[9]). We will leave it to others to present, debate and defend Degrowth as an emancipatory project and social movement toward a post-capitalist mode of living and being in nature.[10] The theory of the Social Ecology of Capital is a prior and more limited endeavor, it provides a framework to critically examine the workings, both material and social, of that which we seek to overcome. It offers a dialectical perspective on the ecological relations of social formations that avoids the pitfalls and reductionism of both idealist constructivism and naturalism. We have sketched a general survey of the metabolic relations developed by capitalist economies, but still much more could be examined, the framework outlined in this inquiry could be

---

8. Bengi Akbulut, "Degrowth," *Rethinking Marxism: A Journal of Economics, Culture & Society* 33(1) (2021): 98–110, https://doi.org/10.1080/08935696.2020.1847014.

9. This has been the approach developed over the years by the Monthly Review school thanks to the pioneering work of John Bellamy Foster and Paul Burkett. For a recent synthesis, see Alejandro Pedregal and Juan Bordera, "Toward an Ecosocialist Degrowth: From the Materially Inevitable to the Socially Desirable," *Monthly Review* 74(2) (2022): 41–54, https://doi.org/10.14452/MR-074-02-2022-06; as well as Michael Löwy, Bengi Akbulut, Sabrina Fernandes and Giorgos Kallis, "For an Ecosocialist Degrowth," *Monthly Review* 73(11) (2022): 56–58, https://monthlyreview.org/2022/04/01/for-an-ecosocialist-degrowth/.

10. Matthias Schmelzer, Aaron Vansintjan and Andrea Vetter, *The Future is Degrowth: A Guide to a World Beyond Capitalism*. London: Verso, 2022.

enriched and amended by the study of the many accumulation frontiers at the point of extraction and at the point of dissipation developed the world over, present, past and future.

This need not be a strictly scientific project; on the contrary, the social forces driving the capitalist treadmill of growth, faced with the imperative of climate change mitigation, are scrambling to find ways to transform the metabolic foundations of advanced capitalist economies all the while preserving its social relations of accumulation, exploitation and externalization. Particularly pressing is the race to try and replace, in the advanced capitalist core, every dirty fossil-based joule in the energy system, with a clean, renewable or biomass-based joule. Serious research by industrial ecologists has shown that this may be possible for some countries but in no way could it be universalized and even limited to the advanced capitalist core, such an intense energy transition would have a devastating impact on biodiversity and might actually gobble up what is left of the planet's carbon budget, burning fossil fuels to build up renewable energy infrastructures. Yet the capitalist sirens of techno-optimism, backed with the social capacity to monopolize investment in future means of extraction, production and consumption, is pushing the social ecology of capital toward new accumulation frontiers which are opening up new socio-ecological struggles. These sirens, promising to preserve and enhance privileged ways of living in the advanced capitalist core and among middle classes in the global south also have their equivalent among those progressives that have bought into the illusion that we can continue growing the forces of production and the throughput, that purer, denser and cleaner forms of energy exist in abundance in an "out there" that remains to be found. So, if, as argued in the introduction, social ecology is a language proposed for those who are challenging the material development of capitalist society, it is also language for those who wish to resist and contest the sirens of progressive eco-modernism and technological accelerationism. It is a language for those seeking to build and embrace a new organic social metabolism amid the ruins of fossil capital, its artifacts and broken promises of emancipation from materiality.

Index

fig refers to a figure; *n* to a note